LUMBERING SONGS FROM THE NORTHERN
WOODS /
C1970.
100101024852017 CENT

CENTRAL C.1
CLOSED STACKS
784.4

Fowke, Edith Fulton, 1913- comp.
Lumbering songs from the northern woods, by Edith Fowke. Tunes transcribed by Norman Cazden. Published for the American Folklore Society by the University of Texas Press [1970]
xiii, 232 p.
(Publications of the American Folklore Society. Memoir series, v. 55)

Unacc. melodies. Bibliography: p. 221-228.

1.Lumbermen-Songs and music. 2.Folk-songs, Canadian-Ontario. I.American Folklore Society. Memoirs, v. 55 (Series) II.Title

784.4'06 GR1.A5 vol. 55
75-107389

LUMBERING SONGS
from the Northern Woods

Publications of the American Folklore Society
MEMOIR SERIES
Wm. Hugh Jansen, General Editor
Volume 55   1970

LUMBERING SONGS
from the Northern Woods

by EDITH FOWKE

Tunes Transcribed by Norman Cazden

C.1c

PUBLISHED FOR THE AMERICAN FOLKLORE SOCIETY BY
THE UNIVERSITY OF TEXAS PRESS, AUSTIN & LONDON

Standard Book Number 292-70018-0
Library of Congress Catalog Card Number 75-107389
Copyright © 1970 by the American Folklore Society
All Rights Reserved
Printed in the United States of America

To all the singers who so generously
shared their memories with me.

ACKNOWLEDGMENTS

I wish to thank Kenneth S. Goldstein, E. C. Beck, Father Joseph E. Gravelle, Mrs. Rae Korson, Joseph Hickerson, Dr. Carmen Roy, Miss Jeanne Monette, and Leslie Shepard, who gave me useful information, and Wm. Hugh Jansen, who was very helpful in editing the manuscript. Thanks are also due to Vera Johnson, who taped Stanley Botting's songs for me; Neil Broadfoot, who supplied Joe Townsend's "MacDonald's Camp" song; Lorne Gardiner, who sent me Mr. Beilhartz's "All Over the Ridges"; and Mr. R. T. Wright, who allowed me to use "Holmes Camp."

I am especially grateful to Norman Cazden, who not only transcribed the music in his usual meticulous style but also provided comments on each tune and supplied extensive lists of tune relatives which will make this book more valuable to musicologists.

The songs from my collection that have been deposited in the National Museum of Canada are published with the permission of the Director of the Museum. The title-page photograph is used through the courtesy of the Ontario Archives.

CONTENTS

DEATH IN THE WOODS

THE LIGHTER SIDE

THE SHANTYBOY AND HIS GIRL

L'ENVOI

LUMBERING SONGS
from the Northern Woods

Introduction

As I noted in *Traditional Singers and Songs from Ontario*, the lumbercamps played a major role in preserving and spreading folk songs of all kinds in this part of Canada. It is not surprising, then, that lumbering should have inspired the largest group of native songs to be found in Ontario and adjoining regions of Quebec. This book is designed to show the wealth of such songs that survived in the memories of former shantyboys.

Collectors in Maine, New Brunswick, and Michigan have published many lumbering songs, but their books also include more general songs popular in the bunkhouses. Because the shantyboys sang everything from old British ballads to American music-hall ditties, it seems wise to limit the term "lumbering songs" to those that describe lumbering or feature lumbering men. Such songs, taken together, give a vivid picture of life in the woods before the days of mechanization.

I do not intend to give a detailed account of the life of the shantyboys, for such information may easily be found elsewhere. Both Franz Rickaby and William Doerflinger have given descriptions of lumbering terms and the processes involved, and the songs themselves are more graphic than any words of mine. However, a few comments on lumbering in central Canada may help to set the songs in perspective.

When the first settlers made their way to the region that is now Ontario, they found the vast territory almost completely covered with primeval forests. The trees were of infinite variety, ranging from chestnut and magnolia through sugar maple, black cherry, and walnut to hickory, blue beech, and white oak. Most important of all, between the Ottawa River and Georgian Bay, the sandy plains that were once covered by the vanished Lake Algonquin bore magnificent stands of white and red pine—the most prized of forest trees. Today we can hardly imagine their size: white pines sold for masts were often a hundred feet long and three feet in diameter at one-third of the way up the trunk. One giant is said to have been eleven feet across at six feet above the ground.

Until the British took over Canada in 1763, these great forests were scarcely touched. Twice, in 1763 and 1775, the British government instructed the governors of Quebec to secure all existing stands of Canadian oak (to be used for hulls) and pine (for masts) for the exclusive use of the Royal Navy. However, plans to reserve timberland for the Crown were never carried out systematically in Ontario.

The first settlers were also the first lumbermen: the land had to be cleared before it could be planted. Some of the United Empire Loyalists who after the American Revolution came to settle along the St. Lawrence began shipping timber to London, and in 1790 Samuel Sherwood took the first timber raft from the Bay of Quinte down to Quebec.

The real boom in Canadian lumbering came when Napoleon's Continental Blockade cut off Britain's trade with the Baltic countries and forced her to look to Canada's forests for timber for her navy. Fostered by preferential tariffs, lumbering quickly became the major industry along the Ottawa Valley. In 1806 Philemon Wright drove the first raft from the banks of the Gatineau to Quebec—a trip of thirty-five days. By 1823 it had been cut to twenty-four hours, and over three hundred rafts made the trip. By 1835 shantyboys were cutting the pine around Lake Timiskaming, four hundred miles up the Ottawa.

To engage in the timber industry, a lumberman had first to secure a limit from the government—though many simply trespassed on Crown lands. The system of issuing licenses was rather casual: in the early days anyone could get a timber berth by sending to the Crown timber office an application enclosing a surveyor's plan and a year's ground rent of a dollar per square mile. Timber limits ranged from ten square miles to one hundred or more. Many lumbermen made fortunes, but the shantyboys never became rich. In the 1890's the going wage as set out in one contract was "not less than $12.00 or more than $18.00 per month," and a teamster providing his own horses and wagon was lucky to earn a dollar a day.

Until about 1870 most of the wood shipped to Britain was in the form of square timber of pine or oak, although quite a few tall trees were exported for masts. The squared timber could be loaded on ships with less waste of space, but the rough squaring of the logs wasted nearly a quarter of the wood and left the forests covered with chips and debris.

On the major rivers the raftsmen build huge drams or floats containing five hundred logs, put together in three layers with oak interspersed among the more buoyant pine and protected with frames fastened together with wooden pins and cross-pieces. Sometimes ten drams would be joined to form one huge raft worth as much as $170,000. The loggers built shanties on the rafts and slept and ate on them as they guided them down to Quebec, using sails or oars, as wind and current determined. On narrower rivers the drams were replaced by smaller units known as cribs, twenty to forty logs laid side by side and fastened together by a frame. A raft of cribs could be broken up to pass over rapids, and occasionally the cribs would have to be broken down into individual logs.

During the 1850's Canada began selling more timber to the United States, and square-timber camps began to give way to logging camps in which the trees were sawed into twelve- or sixteen-foot lengths. At the same time the great timber rafts began to disappear: saw logs were often simply thrown in the river and floated down to the sawmill, sometimes singly, sometimes kept together by large boom logs chained to one another.

Some square-timber camps survived for a few more decades, but by the turn of the century they had practically disappeared. Mr. O. J. Abbott, who worked in one of the last of them, gave me this description:

Well, I remember one time when I worked in a square-timber shanty for awhile, and of course there was a liner and two scorers and a hewer. Well, they used to cut down the tree, and of course, if there was a punk in the tree or anything like that, they wouldn't use the tree; they'd just leave the whole tree there. Sometimes if it was in a square-timber shanty they wouldn't even make a log of it. That's the way it was in the shanty when I was in it—that's a long time ago. Well, they'd fall the tree, and the liner'd line it up, and the scorers would come along and cut a notch off and split the blocks off the side of the tree and then hack it along. And then the hewer would come along and hew the tree, square it, and they'd do the other side, and they'd cant the tree over and make it square. Of course a team of horses had to come along and cant it over—it'd be pretty hard to cant that over with a canthook—and they'd lay it up; and then a man would come along with his team of horses and back up under that and chain it to a sloop, and they'd start off and bring it down to the river and unhitch the chain off it and draw the sleigh from under it and let it fall in the river—and that's the way they used to do.

When I asked Mr. Abbott to describe the work in the regular logging camps, he said,

In a camp where they made them in logs they'd just fell the tree, and they measured it off sixteen-foot long or twelve-foot long or whatever they could make—whatever the tree would make, you know—supposing the tree would make three sixteen-foot logs, or three twelve-foot logs, and they'd cut it off in that. And then the man would come with a team of horses and hitch on a pair of tongs and pull them out and drag them down to the skidway like that, and drive up to the skidway like that, and there was men there to roll them down on the skidway, and they'd pile them up on the skidway until they'd come pretty well on the level of the ground. And then they'd make another skidway in another place somewhere else along the main line. And then when the snow would come they would generally stop making logs and start to draw them to the river. And they had bobsleighs—they had two sleighs what they call bobsleighs—and they'd load them on to them bobsleighs—ten, twelve, fifteen logs—and draw them down to the river. And then there was a man on the river that would unchain them and let them fall on the river, and they were ready for the drive when the ice would go way.[1]

As the decades passed, the center of the industry moved through a series of areas, from the St. Lawrence and its tributaries to the Ottawa and the lower lakes, thence to the Parry Sound and Muskoka regions around Georgian Bay, next to the north shores of Lake Huron and

[1] Taped in Hull, Quebec, October 1959.

Lake Superior, and finally to the Thunder Bay-Rainy River region. Gradually also the rough and ready methods described by Mr. Abbott gave way to modern techniques and machinery, and records, radio, and television replaced the songs of the shantyboys.

Many books detail the history of lumbering in Canada, and those who want further information may find it in such volumes as *Reviewing Nature's Wealth: A Centennial History of Public Management of the Lands, Forests, and Wild Life in Ontario* by R. S. Lambert,[2] *A Hundred Years A-Fellin': Some Passages from the Timber Saga of the Ottawa in the Century 1842–1942* by Charlotte Whitton,[3] *The North American Assault on the Canadian Forest* by A. R. M. Lower,[4] *Hurling Down the Pine* by J. W. Hughson and C. J. Bond,[5] chapter 5 of Edwin C. Guillet's *Early Life in Upper Canada*,[6] and *Up to Date, or The Life of a Lumberman* by George S. Thompson.[7]

In pioneer days Scottish Highlanders are said to have dominated the Ontario lumbercamps, and Ralph Connor gives a colorful picture of their activities in his most famous novel, *The Man from Glengarry*. Although he indicates that they sang many songs, few of them have survived. Almost all the songs still remembered have a distinct Irish flavor. A great many are cast in the familiar come-all-ye pattern (see the Index listing of songs beginning "Come all ye . . ." and "Oh, come all ye . . ."), almost all are set to Irish tunes, and many of the singers had the typical Irish habit of speaking the last word or phrase of a song (indicated by italics in the song texts).

The practice of speaking the last words is so characteristic of the lumbercamp singers that some folklorists have assumed it originated with them, but actually it turns up wherever Irish traditions predominate. Elisabeth Greenleaf notes that it was "a perfectly familiar convention to a Newfoundland audience,"[8] and of course the Irish influence is very strong in the island. James Reginald Wilson writes, "I

2 Toronto: Department of Lands and Forests, 1967.
3 Ottawa: Runge Press, 1943.
4 Toronto: Ryerson Press, 1938.
5 Old Chelsea, Quebec: Historical Society of Gatineau, 1964.
6 Toronto: Ontario Publishing Company, 1933.
7 Peterborough: Times Printing Company, 1895.
8 *Ballads and Sea Songs from Newfoundland*, p. xxxviii.

had always assumed the practice of speaking the last words of a song as being peculiar to folksingers of Miramichi and the northeast," and later notes that "most of the Miramichi tunes are in the Irish folk tradition though many of our singers are of Scottish and English descent."[9] He also mentions that "in the October, 1954 newsletter (*Biblionews*) of the Book Collector's Society of Australia, Professor Brian Elliott reported that Australian folksingers adhere to this practice"[10]—which again is to be expected since most Australian folksongs are cast in the Irish come-all-ye pattern.

Mr. Wilson goes on to speculate: "It is very possible that singers in the British Isles spoke the last words of a song in pre-emigration times. If this is so, we have another instance of a folk tradition being perpetuated in the colonies while dying out in the land of its origin." I would tend to substitute Ireland for "the British Isles" and to qualify the last phrase to read "almost dying out." Certainly the practice has survived better in Canada than in Ireland, but it is still alive there among some singers who represent the older traditions. For example, in his record *Pedlar's Pack*,[11] John Doherty of Donegal speaks the final phrase in his songs "The Three O'Donnells," "Moorlough Mary," and "Rocking the Cradle," as do Willie Clancy of Clare in "The Song of the Riddles" and "The Gander"[12] and Thomas Moran of Leitrim in "Strawberry Lane" and "The Cruel Mother" in *The Folksongs of Britain*.[13]

The shantyboys of central Canada seem to have known almost all the lumbering songs that have had more than a local currency. In my own collecting I have failed to find two that were certainly sung here: "The Shantyman's Life" and "Ye Maidens of Ontario" (also known as "The Maids of Simcoe"). The versions Doerflinger gives of these in *Shantymen and Shantyboys* came from Archie Lant, who learned them in Ontario. With these two exceptions, the singers I recorded knew practically every lumbering song that has been found in more

[9] Louise Manny and James Reginald Wilson, *Songs of Miramichi*, pp. 42 and 286.
[10] *Ibid.*, p. 42.
[11] Issued by the English Folk Dance and Song Society (LP 1003).
[12] Topic 12T175.
[13] Caedmon TC 1145.

than one region, including four ballads that Laws lists as of doubtful currency in tradition (dC 29, dC 33, dC 35, and dC 54). They adapted many existing songs to local situations, and they also sang a great many songs not reported elsewhere. Some of these (notably "The Chapeau Boys," "Anstruther Camp," and "The Haggertys and Young Mulvanny") are excellent examples of the shantyboys' creative talents, and many are sung to fine tunes. In fact, the quality and variety of the tunes clearly refute Stewart Holbrook's comment that "most of the authentic logger songs are dreary stuff. Practically all of them were sung to the same tune and the tune was anything the singer happened to think of—a weaving up and down drone, interminable and, for the most part, lifeless."[14] It is true that some tunes are standard stock, but even these are varied in interesting ways, and the borrowings range from ancient English ballads to American country music.

All of these songs were collected since 1957, and all but three come from singers living in Ontario or just north of the Ottawa River in Quebec. The three exceptions are from British Columbia singers who learned them from Ontario shantyboys. Many of the singers had learned their songs fifty or sixty years ago, and, though they had rarely sung them since, they could still remember them almost perfectly.

The sixty-five titles represent all the different lumbering songs in my collection. I have chosen the best version of the more common songs and given alternate versions only where the song is rare or where the different versions contain interesting variations. Similarly, tunes are given for variants only where there are significant differences. Most of the titles are those used by the singers. Where no title was given, I used the most common title or an arbitrarily chosen identification. The texts are transcribed from the tapes as accurately as possible, although I did not attempt to reproduce dialect pronunciations except for a few characteristic words. Occasionally, where the text is faulty, I have indicated a missing line or supplied an obvious rhyme in brackets.

The songs are grouped into five general sections, although the divi-

[14] *Holy Old Mackinaw*, p. 130.

sion is somewhat arbitrary. Each section begins with the more widely known songs, followed by the local songs that are being printed for the first time. As far as possible, related songs have been grouped together, as well as songs to similar tunes. The text rather than the tune determines whether a song is listed as a separate item or a variant. A few items given separately might have been combined: for example, there is some overlapping in Songs 5 to 9, but on the whole the texts are different enough to justify separating them.

Other traditional versions in print are listed following my comments on each song. These supplementary references are cited by author and page; abbreviated titles are added in citing journals and works by authors for whom more than one entry is listed in the Bibliography. References that Laws cites in his *Native American Balladry* are not here repeated unless they are mentioned in his note; such references appear in parentheses after the Laws listing. Laws' numbers for the ballads follow the song titles.

Recorded traditional versions of a song are listed by record number and singer. Songs that form part of my taped collection of lumbering songs deposited in the National Museum of Canada are not listed in the Bibliography but are identified by numbers beginning with *FO* and come from tapes FO 3, 4, 19, and 20. The Library of Congress Archive of American Folk Song holdings cited are of two types: LP records for sale to the public and Archive discs, usually containing one or two songs, not for sale. The LP records, designated by the prefix *AAFS*, are entered in the Bibliography; the Archive discs, labeled *AFS*, do not appear in the Bibliography. Except for the Library of Congress holdings, I have not attempted to list variants in unpublished collections.

In reference to tune relatives, where the title of the recorded song does not correspond to the title given in the text, the location of the song on the record is indicated by side and band (for example, II–4 means side II, band 4).

Notes on the Analysis of Traditional Song Tunes

Some years ago I proposed that the lumbercamp setting had played a key role in maintaining and transmitting a significant body of traditional song.[1] I suggested that this role went beyond the confines of song text topics of occupational reference; that it accounted for the notable similarity of song repertories found in the Maritimes, in Michigan, and in pockets of lumbering activities, such as the Catskill region of New York State; and that much of the evidence for this distinctive cultural pattern inhered in a common stock of tunes, spread and shared by the migratory workers of the industry. The transmission of strongly similar tunes was deemed especially indicative because new song texts were continually adapted to older tunes, and older texts also were sung to whichever of a number of different tune strains came to mind or was known to the individual singer. The total stock of available tunes nevertheless remained quite well defined and peculiar to the lumbercamp repertory, the song lore of sailing men evincing perhaps the only large spilling over or sharing.

An examination of the gratifying number of pertinent collections of traditional songs published since my article appeared mainly confirms these findings through a wealth of strikingly related tune repertories, with but one notable modification. The statistical analysis I had presented suggested that only a small number of the tunes in question could be traced to prior provenance in English, Scottish, or Irish song, this despite the high proportion in particular of Irish immigrants or

[1] Norman Cazden, "Regional and Occupational Orientations of American Traditional Song," *Journal of American Folklore,* 72 (1959), 310–344.

their immediate descendants engaged in lumbering in eastern Canada and the northeastern United States. Comparisons among the much larger number of individual tunes and their variants now available show that the proportion of tunes that must be ascribed to Irish origin, though by no means dominant in the lumbering repertory, is somewhat higher than my previous investigation could demonstrate. One clear sign of this is the number of parallels to Canadian and United States lumbercamp tunes that have turned up in recently available collections from Australia. It would be difficult to argue any extensive cross-influence in accounting for these parallels; rather a pattern of growth from a common origin would be indicated.

These issues illustrate how the study of traditional song tune repertories may hold intriguing potentials, not only for musical analysis, for which their interest is more considerable than some folklorists even now appreciate, but also for their bearing on historical, anthropological, and sociological studies of cultural processes. Yet to serve these many purposes, it is necessary to establish more firmly the nature of the musical evidence by which comparison is made among tune relatives; for it is not easy to define unequivocally what constitutes the tune to be compared, or which of its features indicate that the tune and its declared cousin both derive from a common parent strain.

The tune, for example, is not the same thing as the precise series of acoustic signals by which it may be registered on sound-recording devices. The tune cannot be that because no subsequent performance of the same song by the same singer will ever exactly match that recorded signal, and neither will the rendering of any one stanza within the song ever duplicate in detail the rendering of another. Yet both singer and listeners will agree that they hear it as the same song, in its several stanzas or on other occasions. We may therefore conclude that the concept of a song tune is a perceived musical entity, somewhat abstracted from and distinct from its concrete acoustic manifestation. Wherein, then, do we locate and grasp this essence or concept of the tune? My opinion is that it comes before us best in the admittedly artificial, incomplete, and schematic representation of the tune in ordinary musical notation.

One excellent guide to discovery of the essence of a tune is Rickaby's statement on how the lumbercamp singer fits different stanzas to it: "One must do as the old singers did: have the melody clearly in mind, then merely juggle the notation in each measure so that the sum total takes care of the whole stanza."[2] The old singers did not, of course, juggle "the notation," save in the metaphoric sense, but my contention is that it is precisely the notated form, subject to the free variation process, that represents the tune itself as we conceive it, that brings it clearly to mind.

Transferring tunes such as those in this collection from their taped originals to staff notation form is thus a far more complex operation than some have imagined, though the mechanics of the procedure is in many respects akin to the taking down of words from oral dictation. The result must be understood as a generalized melody line reflecting some compromise or averaging of detailed differences between stanzas. Some of these differences would emerge at once, should anyone try to sing all the verses to the tune shown.

In the music transcription that follows it is hoped that the generalized form exhibits both the ideal concept of the tune and its most pervasive form of expression. The addenda to the basic tunes show not only the principal variants, but through them the range and manner of variation. As has become customary, each such variant indicates merely the altered version heard of specific measures of music, numbered to correspond to those measures in the basic tune. The metronome indication gives the speed of singing, sometimes within a range of fluctuation or with a gradual increase or decrease of speed within the limits shown.

Many of the tunes have been transposed to a pitch level that is at once simpler to read and in a more common vocal range for most voices. Wherever any transposition has been made, the original pitch of the opening note of the tune is first notated by a key signature and by an initial note that lacks time value. Where two such notes are given, they indicate a fluctuating pitch level of the original or else a gradual change in that level in the direction of the arrow. A figure 8

[2] *Ballads and Songs of the Shanty-Boy*, pp. xxxix–xl.

under the G clef indicates that the notes shown, whether in the catch signature or in the tune proper, are to be understood to signify an octave below the usual G-clef placement.

The method of showing the original pitch level by indicating the initial note is purposely not stated in terms of an original "keynote." To claim the initial note or some other as keynote would prejudge what proper analysis might or might not demonstrate to be correctly the keynote, or to prejudge that there is necessarily such an unequivocal keynote in a particular song, or to prejudge that if there were, the tune would necessarily commence with it. Thus, if a catch signature of the initial pitch level were not deliberately mechanical and hence unprejudiced as to meaning, its showing would in my judgment hinder rather than help us towards proper musical analysis of the tune.

I take a similar questioning view of a procedure followed in certain recent collections, that of setting all tunes arbitrarily in the key of G, for the laudable dual purposes of making them easier to read and easier to compare as related tunes. Such reduction of all tunes to a uniform range and keynote I believe to be neither as helpful nor as justifiable as intended. Indeed I fear it may often mislead the unsuspecting reader seeking tune relationships, for traditional tunes are by no means so regularly or unequivocally in a set key, by the usual standards of musical classification, as always readily to be transposed thence to yield the keynote *g′*. For example, is the tune of Song 41, "The Cold Black River Stream," as notated in this collection to be declared in the key of *g′* as it stands, or is it rather in the key of *d′*?

A more serious impediment to tune analysis appears in many collections of traditional songs, often as the only substitute for careful study of the specific tunes included. That impediment, as I term it advisedly, is the practice of designating mode and genus classifications of the tunes according to the system of so-called church modes, with but slight modification for the purpose. Nonmusician readers and students of such collections have come to expect, as routine tags concealing profound meanings, impressive-looking terms, such as Mixolydian Hexatonic, which they are induced to credit with more precision, usefulness, and pertinence to musical analysis than deserved. Such classifications are deliberately omitted here because they are not in fact applicable, because they are justifiable neither by their historical derivation nor by their practical usefulness, and because they give the illusion of contributing to musical analysis when in fact they impede and mislead.

The applicability of the mode terms Dorian, Phrygian, Lydian, and so on to traditional tunes in collections such as this is historically false, and the terms themselves are symptoms of a fantastic compounding of historical and systematic errors, a thesis I shall develop in detail elsewhere. Here, it is enough to say that the accepted modal scheme for analysis, having outlived its past usefulness and yet having become pervasive in its routine applications, now threatens to disorient the serious student who has to come to terms with the broader lessons of ethnomusicological research. Today that modal scheme mystifies rather than clarifies the cultural history which the study of traditional song ought rather to document. As a result the expressed or implied social outlook of the study has hardly moved beyond the naive, superficial, if charming, romanticism of Cecil Sharp.

A prerequisite for any acceptable hypothesis for classifying traditional tunes would seem to be flexibility of a kind and in a degree that would be impossible for the church mode system to supply. One of the most obvious qualities of traditional tunes is their penchant for turning up in innumerable and continuously variant forms, whereas the nature of the sacred chants required at least an attempt to safeguard a rigidly ordered and changeless ritual.

The accepted mode classifications have proven to be difficult to handle, unrewarding, and notably infertile in the study of traditional tunes. They have not shown themselves fruitful in eliciting insights or in suggesting criteria, let us say, for the contour study Bertrand Bronson seeks or for persistent melodic motifs.

More detailed examination of tunes with the church modes for tools bogs us down even further. Suppose, for example, that in this collection the tune of Song 16, "The Baskatong," is described thus: verse, almost entirely Dorian; refrain, Mixolydian, with uncertain intonation of the seventh; variants of the verse, either Dorian or Mixolydian but with blue-note inflections. How does that help us to compare the tune with its close relative, Song 17 ("MacDonald's Camp"), which we might ticket simply as Mixolydian until we have to account for the low *c#′*? Another version of the same tune-strain is seen in Song 51, "I Went to the Woods," in which the troublesome *c#′* seems to have been obliterated, until we come upon it as an alternate in one variant.

Might these things not be stated more simply without the mode names? Let us state that the tune of Song 16 shows a high sixth degree and a low seventh, while the third fluctuates from predominantly minor in the verse to major in the refrain, and both the third and the seventh show occasional straining toward the higher inflection. Let us observe that the tunes of Songs 17 and 51, like so many tunes, consistently use the low seventh in the upper tetrachord, notably when descending from the keynote, but they consistently use the raised- or leading-tone form of the seventh when it is an auxiliary of the lower keynote.

The approved mode classification would have to dub the tune of Song 61 ("Save Your Money While You're Young") Ionian for the A phrase and (?) Dorian for the B phrase. Thus within a single tune the classification leaps over two legs of Bronson's charming star diagram of intermodal connections.[3] Numerous variants of this tune show a striking persistence of the highly erratic pattern as viewed from the mode definitions. Further, the indicated hedging about the Dorian segment here relates to another inadequacy of the mode principle, for the B phrase is undoubtedly pentatonic in basic structure rather than in any diatonic mode. Whatever analytic terms are decided upon, we would be well advised to have them permit also the clearly standard major form of the same tune, which is given here for Song 42, "Young Conway." Suggestive as well as diverting at this point is the observation that many of the troublesome tunes mentioned above, the song group 16, 17, 51 and the pair 42, 61, which do not readily lend themselves to the older analytic formulas, happen to be of Irish origin.

The church mode classification also suffers from an inability to guide us in regard to the wholly incommensurable principle of scale type or genus, specifically the pentatonic genus that pervades much English, Scottish, Irish, Canadian, and American traditional song. In this collection, the tunes of Songs 12 ("The New Limit Line") and 41 ("The Cold Black River Stream") are unquestionably pentatonic

[3] *The Traditional Tunes of the Child Ballads*, II, xii.

in structure and different in "mode" as well. But just as definitely pentatonic in their basic plan are a number of others—10 ("Turner's Camp"), 18 ("Building a Slide"), 19 ("The Camp at Hoover Lake"), 29 ("Jimmy Judge"), 38 ("The Grand River"), 39 ("The Haggertys and Young Mulvanny"), 45 ("How We Got Up to the Woods Last Year"), and 60 ("Driving Saw-Logs on the Plover"). That aspect ought not therefore to be overlooked merely because they might contain a single incidental leading-tone auxiliary at the final cadence (Song 45), a single or even a repeated passing infix of little rhythmic weight (Songs 18, 19, 29, 38, 39), or perhaps both (Songs 10, 60).

It therefore appears that the accepted mode scheme is too rigid to account for the flexible spontaneous variability of tunes that are transmitted unselfconsciously in oral tradition. By providing the illusion but not the substance of analysis, the scheme fosters a neglect of highly relevant criteria like the pentatonic genus, motif persistence, directional inflected motion, differentiation between stable points and auxiliary ornaments, or the triadic formulas common in European melody.

The intent of this discussion is to propose that, once we free ourselves from the system of modes, the way will lie open to more meaningful and positive approaches. At first it would be inevitable that analysis, to avoid the theorist's penchant for preconceptions, proceed along deductive lines, deriving generalizations from the observed data. Yet as a background to understanding that is not in fact divorced from real history, the musical analyst ought surely to offer tentative hypotheses derived from the wider field of study of musical systems and suggesting at least some initial criteria of probable relevance in the marshaled facts.

Specifically in regard to the tunes in this collection, and to related tunes from the many available documents to which comparison of variants is directed, it is a fair positive generalization that the ground plans of the tunes fall into a variety of modes of the diatonic and pentatonic genera. The diatonic structure of a melody may absorb occasional excursions of chromatic ornaments not included among its normal seven degrees, without affecting the underlying genus because these are heard as alterations. Such ornaments happen to be quite rare in the tradition here considered, and where they occur they serve to indicate the influence of recent commercial entertainment styles and tunes. The pentatonic structure of a melody may similarly absorb occasional infixes, transitions, or ornaments not included among its normal five degrees, also without affecting the underlying genus. Such treatments are relatively common in the lumbering-song tradition, and they are undoubtedly due to the development of pentatonic melody in a cultural environment in which diatonic practice predominated.

A third structure prominent in tunes of this tradition, not usually taken as commensurate with the concept of the genera and yet functioning in much the same way as a ground plan, may be described as a junction of adjacent triads separated by a whole step. Such a parameter does not relate primarily to a harmonic frame for melody as shown in the tonic-dominant-subdominant relationships of recent western art music, or as presently established outside the oral tradition by what may be termed the guitar-picker's syndrome. I refer instead to the older triadic basis indigenous to European (and also to African) melody, in the sense proposed by Curt Sachs,[4] expressed in the pervasive melodic motif of two consecutive thirds, for which the genera in terms of scale do not account. Worth investigating is the fact that traditional tunes like these frequently exhibit as their most prominent formation a triadic structure that moves alternately between two triads on adjacent scale steps. The higher of the two triads is most often minor, though it may be major; the lower is invariably major; and the root of either the higher or the lower may serve as keynote. In this collection the related tunes of Songs 6 ("Hogan's Lake") and 7 ("Hurry Up, Harry") and also 44 ("When the Shantyboy Comes Down") clearly have this underlying structure, the recognition of which seems to have been overly delayed by obsession with church mode precepts to the exclusion of forthright examination.

Yet for all their intrinsic potentials, these intriguing perspectives remain marginal to the crux of my proposal, which can be stated as a principle for the classification of diatonic modes that can be sufficiently pertinent and sufficiently flexible to aid in the study of tradi-

[4] *The Rise of Music in the Ancient World* (New York: W. W. Norton, 1943), pp. 301–306.

tional tunes in a way that the church mode precepts cannot. Some measure of clarity may be achieved if we begin with a description of the operational range of flux, establish within that range some observed crystallization of constants, and then seek to specify the conditions under which one or another constant may predominate or may itself give way to change.

For the diatonic modes it may be observed that several of the degrees composing them appear in alternative values or inflections differing by a half-step, or more rarely by a smaller value. Chief among these inflected positions are the third of the scale, of which the high or "major" form compared with the low or "minor" form determines the important distinction between major and minor character as usually understood. The sixth of the scale may also be either high or low, and similarly the seventh.

The virtue of regarding modal distinctions from the standpoint of variable inflections of high or low versions of the third, sixth, and seventh diatonic degrees in particular, rather than under the seemingly comparable mode schemes of the past, is simply the enormous gain in flexibility, which accords with the freely varying processes of traditional tunes. For example, it permits a direct comparison between the tune of Song 6, referred to above, which uses a minor third, and the obviously related variant tune of Song 7, where the third wavers between major and minor, without requiring a lame statement that the modes are different, which implies a more profound alteration than we observe. The same simplification allows us to compare the tune of Song 16, which I have mentioned uses three species of third, and that of Song 17, its close relative, in which only the major third appears.

Nevertheless, common observation of the tune repertory soon demonstrates that the species of third is a far more constant and stable characteristic of a tune than fixations of the sixth and seventh. A classification of modes according to the high or the low third therefore ought to be regarded as an important and fairly constant criterion of mode distinction, as indeed it is for classical western art music, even while we admit its occasional abrogation, as in the instances just cited. On this criterion we may posit a mode family characterized by a major third, of which variant forms permit a normal or raised fourth, a low or a high seventh, a high sixth but almost never a low sixth, and a high second with never a low second in this particular tradition. A second mode family is characterized by a minor third, of which variant forms permit a low or a high sixth, a low seventh with either sixth, a high seventh not preceded or followed by a low sixth, and, though rarely if ever in this tune repertory, a low second degree.

Historical evidence suggests that for the purposes of a given analysis the distinction between major and minor thirds is primary and other modal values of secondary consideration. In this light it may be useful to classify a given traditional tune, first, on the basis of whether it belongs to the diatonic genus; second, on whether it shows an exclusive or predominant emphasis of a major or minor third; and, finally, according to observed regular or fluctuating treatment of the remaining variable degrees.

The proposed classification assumes a flexible and at times even an erratic treatment of degrees other than the third, whether within a given tune or between variant forms of the same tune strain as sung by different traditional singers. If the singer is apt to regard both a low and a high sixth as equally valid possibilities within a tune, or among different stanzas in his singing of a tune, or if different singers appear to equate such tunes as essentially the same when in fact they vary in such a treatment, perhaps it behooves the well-tempered tune analyst to acknowledge a comparable freedom of alternatives, without having to hide behind the device of a catch-all term like "inflection," which is excluded by a prior rigid scheme of mode definition.

But a hypothesis recognizing the inflected variants as normal rather than as deviations may account positively not only for seemingly unordered variation, but also for regularities of treatment not explicable by the church mode classification. Striking evidence of this principle appears in many of the tunes here in the quite regular appearance of a low seventh as the descending form in the upper tetrachord, but a high or leading-tone seventh below the keynote at the cadence. Examples are listed in the table opposite.

It may be remarked that the high leading-tone seventh turns up typically in measures 3 and 15 of the normal ABBA tunes, thus at the cadences of the A phrase, and I take this for a useful insight. More

Song No.	Title	Measures with Low 7th	Measures with High 7th
13	"Anstruther Camp"	6, 10	3, 15
14	"The Chapeau Boys"	8	14
17	"MacDonald's Camp"	3, 4, 6, 7, 9	2, 10
27	"Jam on Gerry's Rocks"	2, 5, 9, 14	3, 5, 9, 15
34B	"Harry Dunn"	2, 11, 13, 14	3, 15
49	"The Backwoodsman"	2, 6, 7, 10, 11, 14	15
52	"Farmer's Son and Shantyboy"	2 (becoming a 6th in phrase repeat, measure 14)	
61	"Save Your Money"	6, 10	2–3

striking is the observation that in the tunes for Songs 13, 17, and 34B, the treatment of the seventh results in a "mode" utterly impossible by conventional classifications, one which shows consistently a high leading-tone seventh in the lower range of the tune below the key-note but a low seventh in the upper tetrachord. A mode construction whose inflection values change in different octaves is nonetheless quite a reasonable deduction from these examples and, while baffling when evaluated by church mode definitions, follows quite simply from the hypotheses I have offered.

In like fashion it may be reported that the tune of Song 61, "Save Your Money While You're Young," has a major third for its A phrase in measures 1–2–3 and 12–13–14–15 but a minor third in its B phrase, measures 5, 7, and 9. The tune of Song 24, "The Lake of the Caogama," has a more complex differentiation, the minor third appearing in downward motion in measures 1 and 13 and also on an emphasized beat in measures 5 and 9, but a partly raised "blue-note" third replaces it as an ascending weak-beat ornament in measures 6 and 10.

To avoid misunderstanding, it should be added that all of the inflection patterns affecting what I may term the mobile modal degrees are clearly different from the notably chromatic auxiliaries or passing tones occurring in some of the tunes: those of Songs 4 ("A-Lumbering We Go"), measure 11; 54 ("The Gatineau Girls"), measures 3, 11, 19, and its close relative, 56 ("No, My Boy, Not I"), measures 3, 11; and 62 ("You Can't Keep a Shantyboy Down"), measures 2,

4, 10, 12, 24, 26, 28. All of these show derivation from a later "pop" style stereotype of melody that objective field studies are obliged to report as a true functional part of traditional song lore today. The church mode theory of course neither accounts for them nor allows them, and it must be noted regretfully that Cecil Sharp and some other collectors, partly through the bias this fact engendered, sought to minimize or to exclude such tunes from the record.

In brief, I regard the principle of mode classification of traditional tunes according to the accepted church mode doctrines and terminology as a travesty of the musical history both of the tunes and of the theory of modes. Since analysis of the tunes by those precepts also proves faulty and unfruitful in practice and any attempt to apply them tends to frustrate rather than to aid our understanding, it is high time that classification doctrine be discarded and a more resilient criterion established, as deduced from the available data, of which the present collection may be taken as a reasonable sample.

NORMAN CAZDEN

THE SHANTYBOYS AT WORK

1. The Shantyboy's Alphabet

Sung by Emerson Woodcock
Peterborough, Ontario November 1958

1. *A* is for axes, which all of you know,
   And *B* is for boys that can use them also.
   C is for chopping we do first begin,
   And *D* is for danger we ofttimes are in.

REFRAIN

So merry, so merry, so merry are we,
No mortal on earth is as happy as we.
Hi derry, ho derry, hi derry down,
Give the shantyboys whiskey and nothing goes wrong.

2. *E* is for echo that through the woods ring,
   And *F* is for foreman, the boss of our gang.
   G is for grindstone we grind our axe on,
   And *H* is for handle so smoothily worn.

3. *I* is for iron we mark all our pine,
And *J* is for jolly boys always on time.
K is for keen edge all our axes do keep,
And *L* is for lice that keep us from sleep.

4. *M* is for moss we chink in our camps,
And *N* is for needle we mend our old pants.
O is for owl that howl all the night,
And *P* is for pine we fall in daylight.

5. *Q* is for quarreling we do not allow,
And *R* is for river the logs they do plow.
S is for sleighs so stout and so strong,
T is for teams to haul them along.

6. *U* is for use we put our teams to,
And *V* is for valley we run our logs through.
W is for woods we leave in the spring,
So now you have heard all I *have to sing*.

This old woods song, patterned on "The Sailor's Alphabet," is very well known in Ontario as elsewhere in North America. All collections of lumbering songs include it, and most versions show little variation either in the items illustrating the letters or in the refrain. Emerson Woodcock's text is close to the two oldest versions reported, from Maine in 1904 and 1917, and his tune, which resembles "The Wild Colonial Boy," is a good example of the one most commonly used for this song.

REFERENCES

PRINTED. Barry, 50–51. E. C. Beck, *Lore*, 37–40; *Bunyan*, 33–36. H. P. Beck, 265–266. Cazden, *Abelard* I, 12–13. Doerflinger, 207–209. Dorson, *FFMA* 8:1 (1966), 23–29. Eckstorm, 30–32. Flanders *et al.*, 169–171. Flanders and Olney, 112–113. Fowke and Mills, 168–169. Gardner, 255–257. Gray, 10–14. Grover, 197–199. Linscott, 235–237. Manny, 265–267. Rickaby, 35–38. Thompson, 262–263. Tolman, *JAF* 35 (1922), 413–414. Vincent, 44–45. Wilson, 75–76, 93–94 n.

RECORDED. Folkways FM 4052 (Sam Campsall), FM 4053 (Wilmot MacDonald). Library of Congress AAFS L56 (Gus Schaffer), AFS 3709 (Elmer George). National Museum FO 3-30 (Sam Cartwright), FO 3-31 (Mrs. Arthur Hewitt).

TUNE RELATIVES

Barry, 50. Creighton, *SBNS*, 210. Doerflinger, 207. Linscott, 236. Fowke and Mills, 168–169. Rickaby, 37. Wilson, 39 (no. 33).

2. Michigan-I-O (C 17)

Sung by Joe Thibadeau
Bobcaygeon, Ontario October 1964

1. 'Twas in the city of Toronto in eighteen ninety-two
   I met with Isaac Colbourne, a lumberman you know.
   He said, "My hearty good fellows, how would you like to go
   And spend a winter lumbering in Michigan-I-O?"
2. [To him I quickly made reply and unto him did say:]
   "Me going out to Michigan depends on what you pay.
   Oh, if you'll pay good wages and pay our passage out [to and fro],
   Perhaps I'll go along with you to Michigan-I-O."
3. 'Twas on those conditions he 'listed quite a train,
   Full thirty-five or forty, all able-bodied men.
   Our passage being pleasant on the way we had to go
   Till we arrived in Saginaw in Michigan-I-O.
4. Oh, now our voyage is over, and hardships they've begun,
   When Gunther our right agent came boldly rolling in.

He led us to a wilderness, a place we did not know—
'Twas on St. Louis' railroad, in Michigan-I-O.

5. The hardships that we saw that winter would break the heart of man.
To give a full description I'll do the best I can.
Our food the dogs would bark at, and our beds lie on the snow—
My God, there was no bigger hell than Michigan-I-O!

6. So now the winter's over, and hardships they're all done,
And in this cursèd country no longer we'll be found.
When I get back to Canada I'll tell others not to go
To that God-forsaken country called Michigan-I-O.

This account of a shantyboy's suffering dates from 1854, when a Maine lumberman, Ephraim Braley, described a hard winter in Three Rivers, Quebec, in a song he called "Canaday-I-O," patterned on an older English sea ballad, "Canada I O." Further west it became "Michigan-I-O" and "Colley's Run-I-O," and down in Texas it served as a model for "The Buffalo Skinners." It is not common in Ontario: I have recorded only one other version. Joe Thibadeau's tune has been used for the song in Michigan, but he gives it an extravagant treatment at the end of the third line of each stanza.

REFERENCES

PRINTED. Laws, *NAB*, 155. Vincent, 52–53.
RECORDED. Library of Congress AAFS L28 (L. Parker Temple), AAFS L56 (Lester Wells). National Museum FO 3-32 (George Hughey).

TUNE RELATIVES

Barry, 76. Creighton, *SBNS*, 6. Creighton and Senior, 156. Korson, 343. Manny, 120, 137, 187. Petrie, nos. 1243, 1244, 1245. Rickaby, 41. Thorp, 213, 214.

3. The Falling of the Pine

(To the tune of Song 60.)

Sung by Martin McManus
Peterborough, Ontario June 1957

1. Oh, your Irish hearts are wanton,
Your golden hearts are daunten,
To prepare and go to shanty
Before your youth incline,
For spectators they will thunder;
They'll gaze on you and wonder
How noisy is the thunder,
The falling of the pine.

2. It is E. P. took the block,
And we will chop through every rock,
And those owls and wolves are shocked
At the falling of *the pine.*

Fanny Eckstorm notes, "Excepting only the 'Lines upon the Death of Two Young Men,' dated 1815, 'The Falling of the Pine' is the oldest woods song known." She thinks it dates from about 1825. It probably originated in Canada, for most versions speak of running rafts down to Quebec. In addition to Maine, it has been reported only from Michigan and Pennsylvania. This fragment, all I have found in Ontario, was sung to the tune used for "Driving Saw-Logs on the Plover."

REFERENCES

PRINTED. E. C. Beck, *Lore,* 98–99. Dean, 73–74 (reprinted in Rickaby, 82–84). Eckstorm, 17–20 (reprinted in Barry, 18–19). Shoemaker, 197–199.

RECORDED. Folkways FM 4052 (McManus). Library of Congress AAFS L56 (Lester Wells).

4. A-Lumbering We Go

Sung by Stanley Botting
Naramata, British Columbia February 1958

1. Come all ye sons of freedom throughout old Michigan,
   Come all ye gallant lumbermen, come list to a shantyman.
   From the banks of the Muskegon where the rapid waters flow
   We'll range the wildwoods o'er while a-lumbering we go.

2. The music of our burnished axe shall make the woods resound,
   And many a lofty ancient pine will tumble to the ground.
   At night around our shanty fire we'll sing while rude winds blow—
   Oh, we'll range the wildwoods o'er while a-lumbering we go.

3. I am a jolly shantyboy, as you will soon discover.
   To all the dodges I am fly, a hustling pinewoods rover.
   A peavey hook it is my pride, an axe I well can handle—
   To fell a tree or punch a bull get rattling Johnny Randle.

4. I met a girl in Saginaw, and she lives with her mother,
And I defy all Michigan to find such another.
She's tall and slim, her hair is red, her face is plump and pretty.
She's my daisy Sunday-best-day girl, and her front name stands for Kitty.

5. I took her to a dance one night. A mossback gave the bidding,
Silver Jack he bossed the shebang, and big Dan played the fiddle.
We danced and drank the livelong night with fights between the dancing,
Till Silver Jack cleaned out the ranch and set the mossbacks prancing.

6. Oh, the forests so brown at our stroke go down, and cities spring up where they fell,
While logs well run and work well done is the story the shanty-boys tell.

(*The last two lines are sung to the first phrase of the tune: AA.*)

"A-Lumbering We Go" is an interesting welding of two old woods songs. The first two stanzas come from an eight-stanza Maine song originally known as "The Logger's Boast," which was first printed in 1851 and later spread to New York, Pennsylvania, and Michigan. The rest comes from a quite different song usually identified as "Bung Your Eye." Both are rare in tradition, though they have often been reprinted. Stanley Botting said he learned the song from an Ontario lumberman named Charlie McLaughlin. It is possible that Mr. McLaughlin got it from *The Blazed Trail*, by Stewart Edward White, where the two stanzas of "The Logger's Boast" and the three stanzas of "Bung Your Eye" are given separately but in almost exactly this form.

The tune is not memorable, but no other is quite like it. It begins like a tune sometimes used for "The Jam on Gerry's Rocks" and then wanders into a chromatic pattern characteristic of vaudeville music.

REFERENCES

PRINTED. E. C. Beck, *Lore*, 29–32 (reprinted in *Bunyan*, 106–109; Lomax, *U.S.A.*, 166–167). Shoemaker, 80–82. Springer, 132–133 (reprinted in Barry, 14–15; Carmer, 59–60; Eckstorm, 41–43; Gray, 18–21; Rickaby, 219). Thompson, 282–283. Vincent, 34–35. White, 269.

RECORDED. Folk Legacy FSA 15 (Older). Folkways FH 5210 (Seeger). Library of Congress AAFS L56 (Carl Lathrop), AFS 4169 (Lewis Winfield Moody), AFS 3726 (Elmer George), AFS 2308 (Lester Wells).

For "Bung Your Eye" see E. C. Beck, *Bunyan*, 189–190, and White, 260 (reprinted in Lomax and Lomax, *American Ballads*, 450–451, and *Cowboy Songs*, 252–253; and Rickaby, 127–128).

TUNE RELATIVE

Rickaby, 11.

5. The Lumbercamp Song

(To the tune of Song 6.)

A "The Jovial Shanty Boy"
Sung by Emerson Woodcock
Peterborough, Ontario September 1962

1. Come all you jolly boys, I will sing to you a song.
'Tis all about the shanty lads and how they get along.
They're a bunch of jolly fellows so merrily and so fine,
And they spend a pleasant winter in cutting down the pine.

2. The choppers and the sawyers, they lay the timber low.
The skidders and the loaders, they haul it to and fro.
So early in the morning the chore boy he will shout:
"Hurrah! Here, you teamsters, it's time that you were out."

3. The teamsters they'll get up all in a fearful way.
One says, "I've lost a shoepack"; a sock has gone astray.
The loaders they'll get up, their sock they can't find—
They'll blame it on those teamsters and curse them in their mind.

4. So it's snap, crack, goes my whip! I whistle and I sing.
I sit upon my timber sleigh as happy as a king.
My team is always ready; for me I'm never sad.
Oh, who could live a happier life than a jovial shanty lad?

B "A Jolly Shanty Lad"
Sung by George Hughey
Peterborough, Ontario March 1957

1. Snap, crack, goes my whip! I whistle and I sing.
I sit upon my timber sleigh as happy as a king.
My horse is always willing; as for me I'm never sad.
There's no one as happy as a jolly shanty lad.

2. Noon time rolls around, the foreman he will say:
"Lay down your saws and axes and haste to pork and beans."
Arriving at the shanty, the splashing does begin—
The rattling of the water pails, the banging of the tins.

3. Dinner being over, the foreman he will say:
"Time for the woods, my boys,
We'll all put on our coats and caps and haste away
. . . ."

C "Jack the Shanty Lad"
Sung by Martin Sullivan
Nassau, Ontario June 1957

1. Come all you good fellows, I'll sing to you a song.
It's all about the shantyboys and how they get along.
They're a merrily lot of fellows, so merrily and so fine,
Back in the wildwoods a-cutting down the pine.

2. There's the farmer and the sailor, likewise mechanics too.
Takes all kinds of tradesmen to form a lumbering crew.
The choppers and the sawyers, they lay the timber low;
The swampers and the teamsters, they draw it to and fro.

3. Along comes the teamsters just at the break of day:
"Load up your sleds ten thousand feet, to the river haste away
. . . .
. . . ."

4. Snap, sharp goes my whip, a whistle and a song.
My team they are willing, for I am never sad—
My team they are willing, for I am never sad,
For no one leads a happier life than Jack the shanty lad.

D "The Shantyboys in the Pine"
Sung by Jim Harrington
Ennismore, Ontario September 1957

1. Come all my jolly young men, I'll sing to you a song.
It's all about the shantyboys and how they get along.
They are as jolly a crew of boys as ever you would find;
They spend the winter pleasantly a-working in the pine.

2. The farmers' sons they leave their homes, their friends they love so dear,

And into the lonesome pine woods their pathway they do steer.
There's tinkers and there's tailors, likewise mechanics too—
Takes all sorts of tradesmen to form a lumbering crew.

3. The choppers and the sawyers, they lay the timber low;
The skidders and the swampers, they haul it to and fro.
In come the loaders with their teams just at the break of day:
"Hurray, me boys, get on your loads, and haste to clear away."

These four texts, sung to the same tune as "Hogan's Lake," represent one of the most widespread lumbering songs—so general, in fact, that it may be called "The Lumbercamp Song." It probably originated in Maine or New Brunswick, but it turns up in much the same form in nearly every collection from the northeastern states and eastern Canada, under such titles as "Cutting Down the Pine," "Jim Porter's Shanty Song," "Jim Murphy's Camp," and so on.

It was obviously widely known in Ontario in earlier days but is no longer fully remembered. The four fragmentary texts given illustrate what happens when a song begins to break down in oral circulation, and they also show clearly the relationship between the lumbering song and its ancestor, the English music hall song "Jim the Carter Lad."

References

PRINTED. E. C. Beck, *Lore*, 100–107; *Bunyan*, 92–102. Cazden, *Abelard* I, 8–10. Doerflinger, 210–211. Eckstorm, 25–27. Flanders and Olney, 141–143. Gardner, 260. Gray, xvii. Greenleaf, 321–322. Peacock, 750–751 (cf. 'The Herring Gibbers," 132). Rickaby, 69–75. Shoemaker, 90–93 (reprinted in Korson, 350–351).

RECORDED. Folkways FH 5323 (Ives). Library of Congress AAFS L56 (Bill McBride, "Johnny Carroll's Camp"). National Museum FO 3-26 (Hughey), FO 3-27 (Sullivan), FO 3-28 (Harrington).

For "Jim the Carter Lad" see Greig, xcix; Henry, no. 171; Caedmon TC 1144 (Jack Goodfellow).

6. Hogan's Lake

Sung by O. J. Abbott
Hull, Quebec August 1957

1. Oh, come all you brisk young fellows that assemble here tonight,
 Assist my bold endeavors while these few lines I write.
 It's of a gang of shantyboys I mean to let you know,
 They went up for Thomas Laugheren through storm, frost, and snow.

2. 'Twas up on the Black River at a place called Hogan's Lake
 Those able-bodied fellows went square timber for to make.
 The echo of their axes rung from shore to shore—
 The lofty pine they fell so fast, like cannons they did roar.

3. There was two gangs of scorers, their names I do not mind.
 They ranged the mountains o'er and o'er their winter's work to find.
 They tossed the pine both right and left, the blocks and slivers flew—
 They scared the wild moose from their yards, likewise the caribou.

4. Our hewers they were tasty and they ground their axes fair—
They aimed their blows so neatly I am sure they'd split a hair.
They followed up the scorers, they were not left behind—
To do good work I really think all hands are well inclined.

5. Bill Hogan was our hewer's name, I mean to let you know—
Full fourteen inches of the line he'd split with every blow.
He swung his axe so freely, he done his work so clean,
If you saw the timber hewed by him, you'd swear he used a plane.

6. Tom Hogan was our foreman's name, and very well he knew
How to conduct his business and what shantyboys should do.
He knew when timber was well made, when teams they had good loads,
How to lay it up and to swamp it out, and how men should cut the roads.

7. At four o'clock in the morning the teamsters would awake.
They'd go out and feed their horses; then their breakfasts they would take.
"Turn out, me boys," the foreman cries when each horse is on the road,
"You must away before 'tis day, those teams for to unload."

8. If you were in the shanty when they came in at night,
To see them dance, to hear them sing, it would your heart delight.
Some asked for patriotic songs; some for love songs did call.
Fitzsimmons sung about the girl that wore the waterfall.

This ballad from square-timber days resembles the large group of songs that describe the daily routine in a lumbercamp but is distinctive enough to be considered a separate song. Only the seventh stanza of "Hogan's Lake" approximates the other songs using the same tune, whose texts are more general and include many similar lines. "Hogan's Lake" gives a vivid and accurate description of work in a square-timber camp and catches the spirit of the rugged north country, where wild animals roamed the woods.

Canada has many Black Rivers, but "Hogan's Lake" is probably on the one that flows into the Ottawa River just north of Pembroke. Thomas Laugherin was probably Daniel McLachlin, a well-known timber contractor of the Ottawa Valley who died in 1872. "The Girl That Wore the Waterfall" was a popular nineteenth-century song.

The distinctive tune was used for the Great Lakes ballad "The *Bigler's* Crew" and for an English fishing song, "The Dogger Bank," as well as for the many lumbercamp songs.

References

PRINTED. Fowke and Mills, 174–175 (same as above).
RECORDED. Folkways FM 4052 (Abbott).

Tune Relatives

Cazden, *Abelard* I, 8 and 111 references. Creighton, *MFS*, 141, 144. Fowke, 142 (and Folkways FM 4018, II–6). Hugill, 299. Peacock, 132, 750. Folkways FG 3507 (I–1c).

7. Hurry Up, Harry

Sung by LaRena Clark
Ottawa, Ontario August 1965

1. Come all you true-born shantyboys and listen unto me,
   And when that e'er a woodsman that you may chance to see.
   We are a merry set of boys, so handsome, young, and fine,
   And spend a jolly winter a-cutting down the pine.

Refrain

So it's hurry up, Harry, and Tom or Dick or Joe,
And you may take the pail, boys, and for the water go.
In the middle of the splashing, the cook will dinner cry,
And you'd ought to see them hurry up for fear they'd lose their pie.

2. There's blackstrap molasses, squaw buns as hard as rock,
Tea that's boiled in an old tin pail and smells just like your sock.
The beans they are sour, and the porridge thick as dough—
When we have stashed this in our craw, it's to the woods we go.

3. A-hitching up our braces and a-binding up our feet,
A-grinding up our axes for our kind is hard to beat!
A-shouldering up our crosscut saws and through the woods we go—
We make a jolly set of boys a-trudging through the snow.

4. So deeply in the tree of pine we notch to guide its fall,
And not a man among us but will hear the timber call;
And when it crashes to the ground, we'll fall to with a will,
A-trimming up the branches and a-swearing fit to kill.

5. Arriving at the shanty, wet, tired, and with wet feet,
We all take off our socks and boots our supper for to eat.
At nine o'clock or thereabout into our bunks we'll crawl
To sleep away the few short hours until the morning call.

Another offshoot of "The Lumbercamp Song," this is closer than "Hogan's Lake" to other members of the family but yet is sufficiently distinctive to merit a separate listing. "Hurry Up, Harry" seems to be the only song of its type with a refrain, and though it uses several familiar lines in the refrain and in the first and last stanzas, the remaining stanzas are fresh and colorful. It is one of many lumbering songs that LaRena Clark learned from her father and grandfather.

8. Trimble's Crew

(To the tune of Song 6.)

Sung by Calvin Kent
Haliburton, Ontario May 1965

1. Oh, it's of a pair of jobbers who had a jolly time
All in some old log shanty where the jobbers settle down.
All in some old log shanty these jobbers settle down;
It was in this old log shanty with the trees all close around.

2. First they started cutting and then began to skid,
And then they got a fat man who was very like a kid.
The time went on, the job went well, till hunting season came,
And Eddie took his rifle and he went to look for game.

3. It was early Tuesday morning they started with rejoice,
The tall man, the fat man, the teamster, and his horse.
They skidded on the skidway twenty-five or more.
The teamster he got angry, and he jumped, he cursed, and swore.

4. He went out to the jobber, these words to him did say:
"I'm going home this very night and now I want my pay."
The jobber didn't hesitate but went right down with him
And counted out his money till I heard the man grin.

5. He jumped upon his horse; he was happy as could be.
He licked his nag, he made a din as far as I could see.
Barry Colter is a teamster, the lover of his gin.
He drives a very awkward team: we call them Doc and Min.

6. Now to conclude and finish, this truthful tale I'll tell:
A man who'd work for Trimble might better be in jail.
Some people may laugh at this and say it isn't true,
But if you don't believe me, you just ask the Trimble crew.
It was on the shore of Kushog this song it was composed,
And now you've heard the end of it, and that is how it goes.

This local song describing an operation at Lake Kushog, some fifty miles west of Haliburton, goes to the same tune as "Hogan's Lake." Calvin Kent learned it from Cecil Nesbitt of Coboconk some thirty years ago.

9. Poupore's Shanty Crew

(To the tune of Song 6.)

From the Gavan manuscript copy
Quyon, Quebec November 1966

1. Come all you jolly shantyboys wherever you may be,
I hope you pay attention and listen unto me.
It is all about Tom Poupore and his jovial shanty crew.
. . . .

2. On the twenty-eighth of October in 1884
His jovial crew of shantyboys Black River did cross o'er.
Some of them Black River boys, some of them from Sheen,
Some from the Island and more from Nepean.

3. It's when we got together our numbers were not few,
With Westmeath and Chichester boys to finish up the crew.
Tom Poupore is our foreman, I mean to let you know.
He goes ahead: "Come on, my boys, we'll plow through frost and snow."

4. It's when we reached our journey's end our foreman he did say:
"It's stables we have got to build, and that without delay.
We have got to build a blacksmith shop, likewise a shanty, too,
To hold this gang of shantyboys called Poupore's jovial crew."

5. It is now our shanty it is built, and all is going well,
But I must not forget our cook: the truth to you I'll tell,
For cooking in a shanty is a thing can never be excelled,
But some of our boys eat so much they are too fat to see.

6. We have a fine gang of log-makers the timber to lay low,
With good horses and good teamsters to swing it to and fro.
There's Robinson and Boisvert, the main road teams to load,
And old Mr. Gagnon, he's got to sand the road.

7. Robinson he is our lead, I mean to let you know,
And we were bound to follow him, let him drive fast or slow,
And we were bound to follow him, of our numbers they are few,
Still and all we help to form Tom Poupore's jovial crew.

8. The boys they are the lead of course; they always go ahead.
They're closely followed by the brown drove by a chap called Ned.
Next comes their own teams with logs of every sort,
And Dick White told the teamster that his front chain was too short.

9. The next to come is Tommy Burns, he drives a nice gray spare.
Next comes his cousin Jack with Fox Mag and Red Dan.
Next comes Andrew Poupore with Baldy and big Nell:
If you'd ask him to take another log he'd tell you to go to hell.

10. It's now cold winter is over and spring is coming on,
And in the course of a few days we will all be going down.
It's when we get to Pembroke we will fill our glasses to the brim
And drink a health to Dick White and Tom Poupore's shanty crew.

"Poupore's Shanty Crew" is another of the many songs composed by a gang spending the winter in a particular camp and set to the familiar tune of "The Lumbercamp Song." It used to be popular around Quyon and Chapeau, though I found no one now who remembers all the words. Lloyd Gavan, who sang part of it, allowed me to copy this text from a notebook in which his sister had written it (punctuation has been added where needed for clarity). Sheenborough and Chichester are small towns on the north shore of the Ottawa just above Allumette Island; Westmeath lies on the south shore.

10. Turner's Camp (C 23)

A

Sung by Emerson Woodcock
Peterborough, Ontario November 1958

1. From the town of Kinmount
   I chanced to stray away,
   And I landed up at Gooderham
   At eleven o'clock next day.

2. The place being rough and stumpy,
   I thought it next to hell,
   So I jumped on board the I.B.&O.
   And I went to Tory Hill.

3. It rained all day in Tory Hill
   And left it very damp,
   And at supper time well I arrived
   'Way up at Turner's camp.

4. Four o'clock the cook got up,
   His horn did loudly blow,
   Saying, "Arise, arise, my bonny boys,
   You to the woods must go."

5. Out in the wildwoods
Where there is no time to lurk,
And early the next morning
They sent me out to work.

6. First they put me sawing—
They seen that would not pay—
And then they put me loading,
A-loading the damned old sleigh.

7. While rolling up the top logs,
I being so very green,
You roll the logs and turn the logs,
The likes you never seen.

B

Sung by Leo Spencer
Lakefield, Ontario July 1957

1. It's from the town of Saginaw
That I have strayed away,
And I landed in a town called Clara
About eleven o'clock next day.

2. And it being so stumpy,
I thought it next to hell.
I jumped on board a Stanley's Coach
And went to Isabelle.

3. After dinner was over
I thought I'd take a tramp;
Sure I arrived at supper time
'Way out at Turner's camp.

4. Away out in the wildwoods
Where I had no time to shirk—
'Twas early the next morning
They sent me out to work.

5. First they sent me sawing,
And they found that would not pay.

'Twas then they sent me loading,
A-loading a danged old sleigh.

6. The loading of this danged old sleigh,
I being so awful green,
A-rolling up the top logs
Before I never seen.

7. Our teamster being in a hurry
For to get o'er his route,
'Twas roll the log and turn the log
And cant the log about.

8. When the last log was on the sleigh
To the river he would go,
And the way he made his horses get
I'll tell you was no way slow.

9. You ought to see him drive them,
You'd swear that he was drunk.
He was never known to run a trip
Without hanging on a stump.

10. And when the last log was off the sleigh
To the shanty he would go.
And some would talk of curious things
That happened long ago,

11. And some would sing their favorite songs
To the rest of the jolly crew.
But of all the songs that I love best
Was "Bold Jack Donahue."

12. Oh, Sunday it do roll around,
And the boys they get a rest,
While some will go out visitin'
Dressed in their very best.

13. More would sharpen and file their saws
While others grind their axe,
And more would mend and patch their shirts
And hunt their lousy 'backs.

14. The seventeenth of March rolled round
And the weather getting fine,
The teamsters quit their hauling;
The boys they get their time.

15. The teamsters quit their hauling,
And the birds began to sing.
The boys broke down their rollways,
So I guess that it must be spring.

16. Now the winter it's all over,
And the hard work is all done.
We'll all go down to Saginaw town
And have a little fun.

17. Some will go on Stanley's Coach
While others takes the train,
But if you get there before me,
You can whoop 'er up, Liza Jane.

Of the large group of songs that describe life in a particular camp, this is the best known. Usually such songs are remembered only by the men who were in the camp described, but "Turner's Camp" has had wider currency, probably because the events are typical rather than specific. E. C. Beck, who says it was composed on the Chippewa River in 1871, mentions a dozen Michigan singers who knew it, but he prints only one version (from Bill McBride of Isabella City) in his three books. Leo Spencer's version (the "'backs" of stanza 13 are "graybacks," or lice) corresponds quite closely to that Michigan text, and his brother Bill knew it in substantially the same form. Emerson Woodcock's text is nicely localized: Kinmount in his hometown, and Tory Hill and Gooderham are nearby villages. The I.B.&O. is the Ironside, Bancroft, and Ottawa Railway, which ran through the lumbering region. Joe Thibadeau also sang a localized version, about "Erehart's Camp," in which the boys went down to "'Caygeon" (Bobcaygeon), his hometown.

The Ontario singers all use much the same tune. Mr. Woodcock's is related to a common form of "The Derby Ram."

References

PRINTED. Laws, *NAB*, 158. E. C. Beck, *Lore*, 48–51.

RECORDED. Folkways FM 4052 (Leo Spencer, from a different recording). Library of Congress AAFS L56 (Bill McBride). National Museum FO 3-33 (Bill Spencer), FO 3-34 (Woodcock).

Tune Relatives

H. P. Beck, 267. Brown IV, 234; V, 461. Carmer, 72. Fowke, 14 (and Folkways FM 4051, I–3). Manny, 158, 232. Wilson, 30 (no. 26) and 44–45 nn.

11. The Rock Island Line (C 28)

(To the tune of Song 12.)

A

Sung by Tom Brandon
Peterborough, Ontario October 1962

1. I arrived in St. Louis on April the tenth.
   Three weeks in that city for pleasure I spent.
   While perusing newspapers I happened to find
   Advertisement for men on the Rock Island Line.

2. There's Fenians, Bohemians, Norwegians, and Jews
   All walking down Broadway to see Billy Hughes.
   A chip and a quarter a ticket you'll find
   That will forward you on to the Rock Island Line.

3. I went down to the dock all ready to ship
   On the steampship *Old Eagles* to make the round trip,
   Calculating to reach Saskaholia on time,
   There to deadhead a freight for the Rock Island Line.

4. We reached Saskaholia all on the same day.
   Straight to old Greensworth we then made our way.
   "To take on more men I don't feel inclined,
   For we're loaded with men on the Rock Island Line."

5. I went down to the station next morning at eight.
   It was there that the agent said, "My man, you're too late.
   There's a train that left here at a quarter past nine,
   And it's loaded with men for the Rock Island Line.

6. "But to please your desire I'll do all that I can
   For I see by your face you're a hard-working man.
   Go down to headquarters and there you will find
   Brocky Connor's hotel on the Rock Island Line."

7. We started to work on the first day of May—
   A buck and a quarter I heard was the pay.
   After working three weeks I summed up my time:
   I was scarce out of debt on the Rock Island Line.

8. I left Brocky Connor's, the place of my board,
And shouldered my turkey to welt on the road.
Went working for Crowley, that worthless divine
With his big Number 2's on the Rock Island Line.

9. Now there's old Billy Thomas, you'll all know him well.
For cursing and swearing there's few men excel.
He's a fat-bellied Dutchman from over the Rhine,
And he runs the mud pit on the Rock Island Line.

10. He will stand on the bank, and his teamsters he'll scold:
"Come turn round your horses, now back up and load.
Now do as I tell you or else take your time
And skedaddle to hell from the Rock Island Line."

11. The men struck for wages; the contractor said:
"What damn foolish notions they get in their head!
The work can stand still till the devil goes blind—
I won't raise it one cent on the Rock Island Line."

12. "The grub here is rotten," the men they all said.
"If you work long for Crowley you soon will be dead."
So I'll shoulder my turkey and draw up my time
And bid fond adieu to the Rock Island Line.

B "The Margineau Line"
Sung by Kenneth Fleury
Chapeau, Quebec November 1966

1. I went down to the city for a vacation one day
While a week into the city for pleasure to spend.
While reading the paper I once happened to find
Advertisements for men on the Margineau Line.

2. Oh, there was Dutchmen and Scotsmen and some Frenchmen too—
They were all going down there to work for Bill Hugh.
You could slip in the dollar which ticket you would find
Advertisements for men on the Margineau Line.

3. Oh, we've started to work on the very next day,
While a dollar and ten I've heard was their pay.
Oh, I worked there six weeks and I summoned my time—
I was ten cents in debt onto the Margineau Line.

4. Oh, I shouldered my turkey, took a walk on the track.
I fell in with McGunner, and he ordered me back.
With a smile on his face like an African lion
He said, "You'll strike Number Two onto the Margineau Line."

5. Oh the Chimineau girls, they were charming round there.
There were nights into the weeks that they was constant severe;
There was nights into the weeks that they could combine,
And they made a shindig on the Margineau Line.

6. Oh, we danced till the sweat poured down from our clothes,
And us fair shantyboys we pulled nails from our toes.
Now for singing and dancing there's none can combine
Like the Chimineau girls on the Margineau Line.

Both texts are closely related to the Catskill "Rock Island Line" sung by "Dick" Edwards. Tom Brandon's version, learned from his oldest brother, Jack, gives a more detailed description of the work but omits the final two stanzas about "the charming young belles on the Rock Island Line." "The Margineau Line" is a local adaptation that parallels stanzas 1, 2, 5, 6, 9, and 10 in the Catskill text.

Obviously in the same family are "The Fox River Line," which Helen Creighton says was sung all over Nova Scotia with the words changed to fit the locality, and "The Scantaling Line" from New Brunswick. Two Michigan texts, "The East Jordan Line" and "The Keith and Hiles Line," begin with similar stanzas but are otherwise quite different, and two Newfoundland songs, "The Riverhead Line" and "The Bonavist' Line," show even less resemblance to "The Rock Island Line."

The texts above are sung to the tune used in the Catskills, which is like one Rickaby gives for "The Little Brown Bulls" and which turns up elsewhere for "The Wagoner's Lad" and its many relatives.

REFERENCES

PRINTED. Laws, *NAB*, 160 (Creighton, *SBNS*, 252–253; Cazden, *Abelard* I, 52). E. C. Beck, *Bunyan*, 233–235. Leach, 236–237. Manny, 169–170. Peacock, 768–771.

RECORDED. Folk Legacy FSC 10 (Brandon). Folkways FM 4001 (Warde Ford, "The Keith and Hiles Line"). Stinson SLP 72 (Bob DeCormier).

12. The New Limit Line

Sung by Joe Thibadeau
Bobcaygeon, Ontario October 1964

1. Now we left our own homes, for the woods we were bent—
   The first night in Bobcaygeon with pleasure we spent.
   We put up at Harve Thompson's that night for a time
   Who was hiring teams for the New Limit Line.

2. Now the name of those fellows in 'Caygeon that night
   Was O'Neil, Georgie Ell, Pat Breck, and Jim White.
   Harve gave each a fiver and with them did sign
   For to pay our way through to the New Limit Line.

3. So we left there next morning precisely at eight
   So as to reach Minden before it got late.

Oh, we landed in Minden that night just at nine
With our hearts full of joy for the New Limit Line.

4. There were two other fellows with young Lambert Jack
Who had started with sleighs but you bet they turned back,
But we never halted those hills for to climb—
We're bound to go through to the New Limit Line.

5. So early next morning we were ready again,
But before we reached Dorset met two other men.
They advised us to turn back and to do it in time
For you'll never get through to the New Limit Line.

6. It was on Tuesday evening we reached Gilmour's big mills
After toiling for five days through mud and o'er hills.
Our horses were faggin' with hunger near blind
When we reached the big boarding house on the New Limit Line.

7. There we met with Sam Gunther, our names he did stand.
He gave us an order to Jim Campbell's camp,
Saying, "Go there in the morning, take plenty of time,
For you brought your load through to the New Limit Line."

8. So early next morning we spiked up our bunks
With toggles and sway bars to hold on those trunks.
Then we started to haul, for to haul the white pine,
Till we hauled the last load on the New Limit Line.

9. Our lead was St. Thomas, from Nogies Creek mouth,
But a Frenchman called Sweenor he tried to run him out,
But our Bobcaygeon boys they all got combined—
They ran Sweenor to hell from the New Limit Line.

10. Now Al Booth and Dick Cavanagh were two jolly chaps—
Some teams they'd give hell while more they'd give stance,
But if you were a friend you were sure of the time
For they run the top off the skids on the New Limit Line.

11. They would stand at the skidway and this they would say:
"Now the next man comes Sweenor, we'll make this his last day,

For we'll load him down until he'll take his time,
For he drives a hired team on the New Limit Line."

12. Now a man named Joe Pelletier was our stable boss.
He'd both damn and he'd scold if we let feed go to loss.
Those teamsters he'd scrap with them one at a time
Till he scarce had a friend on the New Limit Line.

13. Now for light-hearted fellows we had plenty in view—
You could tell that our laughs were not rough or subdued.
On week nights or Sundays we all would combine;
We'd dance or shindig on the New Limit Line.

14. We'd dance till the sweat it would smear all our clothes,
While our rough shanty slabs knocks the nails from our toes.
You may search this world over and equal won't find
Than our Bobcaygeon boys on the New Limit Line.

15. Now our logs are all hauled, and we're homeward bound,
And when we reach Dorset this toast will go round:
"Here's a health to Jim Campbell for he used us most kind!
Hope we'll all meet again on the New Limit Line."

Although probably inspired by "The Rock Island Line" and sung to the same tune, this is a quite different song, describing the adventures of a group of Bobcaygeon boys who went to work at Campbell's camp on "The New Limit Line." Like "How We Got Up to the Woods Last Year," it details a trip from home to the camp, in this case from Bobcaygeon, through Minden and Dorset, into Muskoka.

Joe Thibadeau, the only person who sang this song for me, says that his uncle, Louis St. Thomas, helped to make it up and that Dick Cavanagh, Al Booth, Bob Kimble, and Jack Lambert from Bobcaygeon had been on the gang. It resembles many similar songs made up by particular crews but is more detailed and graphic than most. It probably dates from about 1870. Writing in 1871 in *Up to Date or The Life of a Lumberman*, George S. Thompson mentions "Messrs. Gilmour's depot shanty on their new limit in Muskoka, for which limit they paid nearly one million dollars to the Ontario government two years ago." Mr. Thompson also mentions P. M. Gunther, the chief bush superintendent of the firm—probably the Sam Gunther of stanza 7.

TUNE RELATIVES

Beck, *Lore,* 66–67. Brown IV, 209–210; V, 159, 171. Cazden, *Abelard* I, 52–53, 121 n. Creighton *MFS*, 192; *SBNS*, 38. Creighton and Senior, 146. Joyce, *OIFM*, no. 531. Manny, 169, 279. O'Neill, no. 222. Peacock, 882, 963, 998. Folkways FM 4053 (II–3).

13. Anstruther Camp

Sung by Joe Thibadeau
Bobcaygeon, Ontario   October 1964

1. Oh, come all my brave companions, I won't detain you long.
   It's all about last winter I will tell you in my song.
   'Twas in Anstruther township where we were bound to stay,
   And we worked the whole long winter there for very little pay.

2. Archie Patterson was our foreman, a man so young and bright
   He could see daylight coming almost any hour at night,
   And early, early in the morn those words to us would say:
   "Hurrah, my boys, we'll try it now, for it is breaking day."

3. We would start on our weary way through dales and over hills
   Till at length our work we've reached—the stars are shining still.
   Then up would speak our chopper saying, "I think it's rather soon
   For to go and fall the lofty pine, for yonder is the moon."

4. We would all sit down and meditate, think of home and friends so dear,
And wonder what they'd think or say if they could see us here.
Our fathers, mothers, sisters dear, and loved ones home at rest,
We wish we could be with them all, the ones that we love best.

5. Then up would speak our old teamster, these words to us would say:
"You swampers, get that trail up there, one hundred logs today";
While our rollers with their cant hooks neat the round logs they do pile,
And they do their work without complaint and always with a smile.

6. Then at last it comes our dinner time, we gather round the fire
And we eat the good old western pork until our heart's desire.
. . . .
. . . .

7. Then at last the day is over, and our day's work it is done,
Then over that mountainous trail we start out at a run,
Until at length the camp we've reached, the place we call our home,
For the shantyboys we fear no noise wherever we do roam.

8. Then at length the cook calls, "Supper, boys!" We crowd into our seats—
It is a sight for all sore eyes for to see those brave boys eat.
And then the supper it being over, we talk of the day gone by,
And Jack will say to Jim, "Old boy, did you get enough of pie?"

9. So come all you pretty fair maids that gather round me here
To look upon our shantyboys, yes, rather with a sneer,
But if any of you fair young maids would choose to live a life of joy,
Just join your hands in wedlock bands with your roving shantyboy.

(The fragmentary sixth stanza uses parts of the first melodic phrase.)

"Anstruther Camp" is better than most local songs, having some particularly graphic lines. Joe Thibadeau said he heard it from an old-timer in Cavendish camp about twenty years ago and believed that it told of a camp near Buckhorn around 1900. Its tune resembles "The Maid of the Mountain Brow," which was very popular in Ontario.

TUNE RELATIVES

Brown V, 70. Cazden, *Abelard* II, 68. Fowke, 90 (and Folk Legacy FSC 10, I–5); 112–113 (and Topic 12T140, II–6). Greenleaf, 153. Leach, 128.

14. The Chapeau Boys

Sung by O. J. Abbott
Hull, Quebec August 1957

1. I'm a jolly good fellow, Pat Gregg is my name.
   I come from the Chapeau, that village of fame.
   For singing and dancing and all other fun
   The boys from the Chapeau cannot be outdone.

2. On your patience I beg to intrude.
   We hired with Fitzgerald who was agent for Booth
   To go up the Black River so far, far away,
   To the old Caldwell Farm for to cut the hay.

3. Joe Humphrey, Bob Orme, Ned Murphy, and I,
   We packed up our duds on the eleventh of July.
   Away up to Pembroke our luggage did take,
   We boarded the *Empress* and sailed up the lake.

4. When we came to Fort William, the place you all know,
   We tuned up our fiddle and rosined our bow.
   Our silver strings rang out with a clear merry noise,
   And Oiseau Rock echoed, "Well done, Chapeau boys!"

5. We headed for Des Joachims and got there all right.
We had sixteen miles to walk to Reddy's that night,
Where we were made welcome. The truth for to speak,
It was our desire to stay there a week.

6. But we left the next morning with good wishes and smiles,
And the route to the Caldwell was forty-six miles.
North over the mountains Bob showed us the route,
And when we got there we were nearly played out.

7. Now the board at the Caldwell, the truth for to tell,
Could not be surpassed in the Russell Hotel.
We had good beef and fresh mutton, our tea sweet and strong,
And great early roses full six inches long.

8. We had custard, rice pudding, and sweet apple pie,
Good bread and fresh butter that would you surprise.
We had cabbage, cucumbers, boiled, pickled, and raw,
And the leg of a beaver we stole from a squaw.

9. Haying being over, we packed up our duds,
Shouldered our turkey and off to the woods
To fall the tall pine with our axes and saws,
To terrify the animals, the Indians, and squaws.

10. I hope we'll have luck, and on that we rely.
I hope the drive will be out by the eleventh of July,
And if we're all spared to get down in the spring,
We'll make the old hall at the Chapeau to ring.

11. I think I'll conclude and finish my song.
I hope you won't mind me for keeping you so long,
But our cook's getting sleepy, he's nodding his head,
So we'll all say our prayers and we'll roll into bed.

In describing the adventures of a gang of local boys "The Chapeau Boys" resembles "The New Limit Line," but it has had wider currency. In addition to O. J. Abbott's version, I have it from William Dennison, who grew up in Renfrew, and from Lennox Gavan, who lives near Chapeau and learned it from the composer's grandson. I also have an undated print copy from an old newspaper and a copy from the notebook of Gertie Mercier of Foresters Falls, Ontario, dating from 1927. The song can still be heard in Chapeau bars on Saturday nights.

The composer, Patrick Gregg, was a local lumberman and musician. The Reverend Joseph E. Gravelle, unofficial historian of the Ottawa Valley, says that Patrick was the third son of William Gregg and Frances Meehan, who came out from Ireland to settle on Allumette Island in the 1850's. He believes that Patrick wrote the song in the spring of 1869, when he returned from spending the winter in the bush, and notes that he had reason to remember the stop at Reddy's farm, for on September 7, 1869, he married Fanny Reddy.

One of the reasons why the song has been preserved so well is that the composer's grandson, also named Patrick Gregg, was in the habit of singing it at concerts in the Chapeau hall in later years. (Father Gravelle gives many other details about the persons mentioned in the song in an article in *The Renfrew Advance*, January 20, 1966).

The town of Chapeau is on Allumette Island in the Ottawa River just north of Pembroke. The Fort William mentioned is not the city on Lake Superior but a small village on the north shore of the Ottawa. Des Joachims (pronounced locally as "the Swishaw") lies on the Ottawa between Pembroke and North Bay. The Black River runs north of and parallel to the Ottawa before cutting south to join it. John Fitzgerald was an agent for J. R. Booth, a well-known Canadian lumber king. There once was a Russell Hotel in Ottawa, and "early roses" is a country name for radishes.

All texts of the song are quite similar. Mr. Gavan sings stanza 10 as:

> When the drive it is over, I hope 'twill be soon,
> We expect to be down by the first week in June,
> And if God spares our lives to go home in the spring,
> We'll make that new hall at the Chapeau to ring,

and adds an extra stanza:

> Now the boys from the Chapeau can dance and can sing—
> Sure they're just as happy as any emperor or king.

We're seven fine fiddlers: there's none of us drones,
And Michael, my brother, can rattle the bones.

Mr. Abbott's tune shows some relationship to an unpublished version of "The Lady Leroy" sung by George Edwards and is also like the form of "Villikens and His Dinah" used for "Jack Haggerty."

References

PRINTED. Fowke and Johnston, 72–73 (same as above).

RECORDED. Folkways FM 4052 (Abbott). National Museum FO 3-25 (Dennison).

Tune Relatives

See Song 53 and Wilson, 25–27 (no. 20) and 43–44 n.

15. All Over the Ridges

(To the tune of Song 14.)

Sung by Reuben Beilhartz
Bruce Mines, Ontario November 1965

1. All over the ridges we lay the pine low.
   They break in the fall for the want of more snow.
   Says Murphy to Burk, "You're the worst out of jail
   For breaking up timber on Martin McHale."

2. The first afternoon I refused to remain
   In charge of Fred Miller he put me to chain.
   It was at the head of a pitch-off where cold blows the gale
   Where we landed the timber for Martin McHale.

3. Our cook's name's Jack Dunnigan, the best in the woods.
   His beans they are great, and his bread it is good,
   And his elegant sea pie will make quite a meal
   For the boys that are laboring for Martin McHale.

Lorne Gardiner of Sault Ste. Marie recorded this fragment from Mr. Beilhartz, who heard it in his childhood when he lived near Buckingham on the Lièvre River, before moving to the Sault Ste. Marie district in 1904. Burk is a common name in the Gatineau Valley, and Mr. Beilhartz says that Fred Miller was still living near Buckingham in 1905.

16. The Baskatong

Sung by O. J. Abbott
Hull, Quebec   August 1957

1. Oh, it was in the year eighteen hundred and one
   When I left my poor Kate all sad and alone.
   Says I to my Kate, "Sure three months won't be long,"
   But it's little I thought of the Baskatong.

REFRAIN
Laddy fal the deedilero, right fal the dolday.

2. Oh, we had a good foreman, Kennedy was his name.
   To speak bad about him 'twould be a great shame,
   For suckholes with him they had no great sight,
   For he treated all the men in the shanty alike.

3. Old Kennedy's Dan he was jovial and true.
He drove a pair of colts, they were about twenty-two.
He'd drive fast all day and he'd ne'er be out late,
But he thought he'd play hell if Big Jack had a mate.

4. Old Kennedy's Dan he soon gave them a stroke
For the very next morning the harness he broke.
He took them to the shanty and that very fast,
And he told the old man to stick them in his eye.

5. We had a good loader, Morrisette was his name.
To speak bad about him 'twould be a great shame.
He'd lift like a brute when the logs would be large,
Saying, "Up with them, boys! Now lève, Joe Labarge."

6. Oh, one night we had a great talk
About the herrings that taste of the salt,
And the door of our shanty would give you a fright—
We were running up and down to the river all night.

7. I think I'll conclude and finish my song.
I hope you won't mind me for keeping you so long.
I'll write a letter to Kate saying it will not be long
Till I'll be returning from the Baskatong.

I have found only the one version of this song about Lake Baskatong, which lies some hundred miles north of Ottawa. The form suggests that it is an offshoot of the better-known lumbering song about "Moosehead Lake." Here the pattern is a series of jokes about people and incidents, and O. J. Abbott obviously modified the language, notably at the end of stanzas 4 and 6. A less obvious change comes in stanza 5, where he substituted "Now lève, Joe Labarge" for "Mon Christ et sa vierge."

The old Irish tune is used for a comic ballad, "The Poor Countryman," known by George Edwards. It must have been very popular with the shantyboys for they used it also for "MacDonald's Camp" and "I Went to the Woods" (Songs 17 and 51).

References

PRINTED. Cf. "Moosehead Lake" in Creighton, *SBNS*, 265–266; Lomax, *North America*, 115–117; and Lomax and Lomax, *Singing Country*, 226–228. Also "Mel Whitten" in Gray, 60–62.

RECORDED. Folkways FM 4052 (Abbott).

Tune Relatives

Cazden, *Abelard* II, 40–41. Creighton, *SBNS*, 265. Greenleaf, 138. Ives, *Larry Gorman*, 74–75. Joyce, *OIFM*, no. 594. Petrie, nos. 740, 823.

17. MacDonald's Camp

Sung by Joe Townsend
Seaforth, Ontario December 1963

1. One evening last fall when we felt well inclined
   We hired with D. A. MacDonald to work at the pine.
   The place he put us was rougher than blazes;
   It was down at the new base among the hard cases.

REFRAIN
   Singing fal a-ler-ler-dle, il-der-dle, i-lay.

2. Here's for D. A. MacDonald, he was a devil to trot.
   He brought bread seven miles, and he got it here hot.
   When we sat down to dinner we thought we had none,
   But the boss he arrived there before we got done.

3. Here's for our cook, he was as good as gold.
   He left his old father when fourteen years old.
   He hired at D. A. MacDonald for to do what he could—
   For to score at the loaf and to chop at the wood.

4. Here's for James Proudfoot comes next in our song.
If Jimmy don't do better he won't be here long.
At breaking saw handles is Jimmy's delight,
For to get into the shanty long before it's night.

5. Here is for Bernie Knott, he's our swamper you know.
He works very steady but devilish slow.
He cuts his stumps high and he trims his knots long,
And tell him to do better, he never lets on.

6. Here is for young Charlie Proudfoot comes next in our song.
He contracted for a cedar that did not last long.
He got three cents a post, and I think he cut seven.
Success to you, Charlie, I wish you eleven!

7. Here's for Malcolm Montgomery, he roams far and wide.
He spied some long tamarack down by the lakeside.
The place this timber grew it must have been forgotten,
For Malcolm he swears that the half of it's rotten.

8. Here's for Joe Townsend, a fine lad is he.
He drives a gay team, and you all know they're free.
He shoves on the big load, and you hear his whip crack,
And away goes the whiffletrees over their back.

9. Here is to Jack Caldwell, the next in our song.
At rolling the logs he is no use at all.
When he meets a big log he gets a pain in his back,
And then he is ready to ask for the *sack*.

These verses, which Neil Broadfoot recorded from Joe Townsend, use the same tune as "The Baskatong" but follow the more conventional pattern of the "moniker" songs, which name all the men in the crew and describe their jobs. Before singing it, Mr. Townsend, then eighty, said, "This was composed by a man by the name of Jack Caldwell, who worked in the camp. This camp was at a rock-cut near Sioux, Ontario. He was our skidder in that camp. This was about sixty years ago, and horses was the go then—no automobiles, only sleigh rides. This is Joe Townsend that worked in the camp and had a balky horse."

TUNE RELATIVES. See Song 16.

18. Building a Slide

Sung by George McCallum
Grafton, Ontario August 1962

1. Come all you young fellows from near, far, and wide,
   And I'll tell you a story of building a slide.
   It was a bay up in that Wanapitei—
   I think I'll never forget that day.
   Oh, there was Jim O'Keefe, from Nakina he came—
   He has a good head and I'll tell you the same.

There was Rory MacDonald and Jack Donahue,
And Rory O'Keefe from the head of the Soo.

REFRAIN
Oh, it's ho derry, ho derry, ho derry down,
Give a shantyboy grog and there's nothing goes wrong.

2. Oh, there was George McCallum, he drove a pair of bays—
He was drawing out boom timber on the two sleighs.
He was always goin' with a rip and a tear—
He was a good guy, but a terror to swear.
Jack Holmes, our cook, we all knew like a book
For you couldn't eat anything he would cook.
He had cabbage, cucumbers, all pickled and raw,
And the leg of a beaver he stole from a squaw.

3. Now the drive it was down, I think 'twill be soon.
I think we'll get through about the first day of June,
And to tell you the truth, I'll never forget
The day I went up in that Wanapitei.
We all got out to Gorries, we were all very dry.
Says Finner to Bolden, "We'd better drink rye."
And we all consented, we'd drink merrily,
And we all got a bottle of strong Eighty-Three.

Another "moniker" song, "Building a Slide" is set in a more remote area of Ontario, near Lake Wanapitei north of Georgian Bay. Its excellent tune is derived from those used for "The Shantyboy's Alphabet," whose refrain it borrows. It also borrows the last two lines of its second stanza from "The Chapeau Boys." As with "MacDonald's Camp," the singer figures as one of the characters in the song.

TUNE RELATIVES

Leach, 232. O'Lochlainn, 84. Petrie, nos. 387, 1130, 1319.

19. The Camp at Hoover Lake

Sung by Leo Spencer
Lakefield, Ontario   September 1962

1. The first day of September we were all at hand
   For to go to the shanty at Sheehan's command,
   And we left wives and sweethearts to mourn for their sake
   For to go spend the winter up at Hoover Lake.

   So it's shove 'round the bottles for old friendship's sake
   And remember the days we were up on the lake.

2. When we came to the Sound we boldlie stepped in,
And we called for refreshments, which quicklie came,
And the joke it went round without any noise,
And she said she ne'er saw such respectable boys.

3. So it was late the next evening the shanty we spied:
The same was enough to bring tears to your eyes,
For it looked more to me like a nest of mudhens
Than a place of abode for young shantymen.

4. There was Pat Riley and Con Riley too,
Bill Sullivan from Lakefield dressed in navy blue,
And there's Pete McMurray, likewise little Dan,
Leo Whims that courted that fair Kathy Ann.

5. For a month and a half, oh, we got along fine,
A-shaking the balsams and tripping the pine,
Till into our camp the teamsters did flock,
And they tread o'er our corns and stole all our songs.

6. There is McAvalay, he drove the good grays,
And there's Frank McMurray, he drove the big bays,
And there's Gerin Gowland, he drove Chum and Fred,
And it's old Dick Leary drove Donnie and Ned.

7. McMurray drives up to the skidway and says:
"Spencer, load light for she runs hard today."
Then he flung up his chains with a hell of a smash,
And he swore that he'd dump off the logs on the mash.

8. Now the winter is over, the logs they're all down.
And the boys get their cheques, and they're dandled to town,
But to tell you the truth there was none could out-haul
That little Mitunik drove Jerry and Doll.

This song, about a winter spent up near Owen Sound on Georgian Bay, again incorporates the name of the singer, along with those of several other men from the Peterborough area: Bill Sullivan, father of the Martin Sullivan who contributed several songs to this book, and Con Riley, who has also sung for me. Leo Spencer's tune is similar to that of "Building a Slide" and "The Shantyboy's Alphabet" but has parts resembling "The Rock Island Line," which suggests that the singer confused two tunes. Mr. Spencer did not repeat the refrain-like lines following stanza 1 for the remaining stanzas.

TUNE RELATIVES. See Song 18.

20. Hauling Logs on the Maniwaki

Sung by Michael Cuddihey
Hull, Quebec March 1965

1. The twenty-sixth of December the weather was fine.
We started from Logues about half past nine.
We dinnered at the Eagle, 'twas the best we could do.
Said Fournier, "Without feeding you cannot get through."

REFRAIN
Derry down, down, down derry down.

2. There's three miles of the portage is damnable rock.
If it's dark when you get there you'll get it damn tough.
We struck the Little Turtle; 'twas then ten to five.
"Oh, now then," says Fournier, "You'll open your eyes."

3. We shoved round the bottle and took up the hill.
The next two we met were McBoyle and old Bill.
They says, "How are you coming?" Says I, "Pretty tough."
"Oh, yes," said Bill Logue, "for it's damnable rough."

4. When we got to the shanty we bid them goodnight.
There was some of us sober and more of us tight.
Said Fournier, "I'll unhitch," and said Pat, "You're darn right.
We'll unload in the morning when we have daylight."

5. Barry Keegan, Bill Skibas are leads on the sleighs.
One drives the white pacers, the other the bays.
God bless the poor habitants! They'll get it hot—
When they can't follow walking, sure they're asked to trot.

6. One Monday morning we were short of a man.
Pat came out himself for to give us a hand.
The load they went on and the change they did fill—
Young Emory's team backed twice down the hill.

7. When you get to the dump, the unloader is there.
I'll tell you his name: it is young LaFlare.
With his pencils and board your logs he will count,
And every night he has a big amount.

8. The clerk we have here, his name is Moore Dick.
If you waste any hay, he will tell you damn quick.
Every side that you turn, it's a key in the lock,
But Weeniver Kay he keeps oats in the box.

9. Paddy Keeney is our foreman, a devil to rush.
When we should be in bed, we're all out in the bush.
From the dump to the skidway, and that's his whole beat,
Ready to curse every teamster he meets.

Another realistic account of a gang in the bush, this one emphasizes the work of the teamsters, who hauled the logs from the place they were cut to the shore of the lake or river so that they could be floated down in the spring. Michael Cuddihey says he learned the song from J. T. Keeley in about 1912. The Maniwaki is north of Ottawa.

The very old tune, known as "Down, Derry Down," is among the most common in lumbercamp settings, more often sung to texts like that of "Shannelly's Mill" (Song 50). It is also used for "The *E. C. Roberts*," and Rickaby gives it for "The Little Brown Bulls."

TUNE RELATIVES

Bronson I, 354–361. Cazden, *Abelard* I, 102, 116 n. Fowke, 140 (and Folkways FM 4018, I–1; Prestige/International 25014, I–5). Harlow, 189. Hugill, 466. Ives, *Larry Gorman*, 91–92. Leach, 216, 236. Peacock, 136, 368. Rickaby, 65, 161.

21. The Teams at Wanapitei

(To the tune of Song 45.)

Sung by Alex Craigo
Kinmount, Ontario October 1964

1. In eighteen hundred and ninety-five
Away to the woods we thought we'd strike.
We hired with Riggin on the Georgian Bay
To go to work at Wanapitei.

REFRAIN
To me rant and roar and fal the diddle ay,
Rant and roar and drunk on the way.

2. Seventeen miles we walked to the boat,
And then how lightly she did float.
We sailed along, and we kept first rate.
When we got there 'twas damn good and late.

3. And then there was the pine to cut,
And skid them, boys, and skid them all!
And then there was the teams to load,
And bog them on with a damn big load.

4. Oh, the first team in was a pair of bays—
They were the boys could handle the sleighs.
The teamster sits, and he gives a snort.
Says he, "By God, this is no summer's resort!"

5. Oh, the next came in was a bay and a black—
They were the boys that wouldn't hold back
To hear that whip go clickety clack
And the teamster saying, "Now damn you, Jack!"

6. Oh, the next team in was the Pushes' team—
You'd think, by God, they were run by steam.
They run four trips on a four-mile road,
And forty-five logs in every damn big load.

Although Alex Craigo had known many songs in his youth, this is the only one he could remember at the age of eighty, which indicates that it had particularly appealed to him. Unlike many similar songs, it has had more than local currency: in June 1966 I recorded a four-stanza version from Pat and Austin Anderson in Winnipeg, Manitoba.

The tune and the chorus are those of the more widely known "How We Got Up to the Woods Last Year." As in "Building a Slide," the location is Lake Wanapitei, north of Georgian Bay, and, as in "Hauling Logs on the Maniwaki," the emphasis is on the work of the teamsters.

22. The Squire Boys

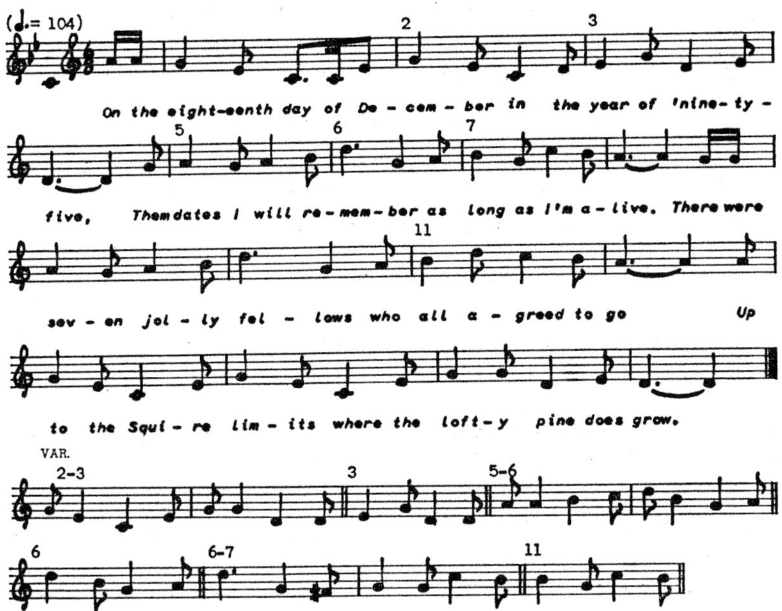

Sung by LaRena Clark
Ottawa, Ontario August 1965

1. On the eighteenth day of December in the year of 'ninety-five,
   Them dates I will remember as long as I'm alive.
   There were seven jolly fellows who all agreed to go
   Up to the Squire limits where the lofty pine does grow.

2. There was O'Meara and Dave McQuin and Ned LaFrance also,
   And one of McGill's teamsters to show us where to go
   On that old frozen river, the ice not very strong,
   But by his careful guidance we slowly moved along.

3. Oh, when we reached the Ottawa, he gave us this advice,
   Saying, "Single out your horses, boys, be careful of the ice,"
   Saying, "Single out your horses, boys, and make them step out light.
   To cross the Ottawa River you're at the trial point."

4. Oh, when we reached the other side, our dread and fear all gone,
We said that no more farther that night we'd travel on—
Up to the Squire dovecote, that little farm so fair—
But early the next morning a camp we would prepare.

5. We met some loaded teamsters on our way going in.
The rain had fell in torrents, and it wet us to the skin.
The first we met was Lester, young man of town and fair,
For to draw logs this afternoon he said you may prepare.

6. "Your sleighs are down upon the road; we passed them coming by.
Two revolutions you must make down through the brewery snye."
Pat Bridgeman was the young man who gave me my first load,
And sorry I am for to say he froze me to the road.

7. The man who was ahead of me, he had still a harder fate.
I said, "Stay here till I come back, and I'll give you a break."
"Go 'long, go 'long now, my kind friend. For me you need not fear.
If my harness stands the pressure, I'll be a short time here."

8. My anxious heart persuaded me my tongue for to keep still.
My courage almost failed me when I saw the brewery hill.
Bill Dempsey, our unloader, born on this wild stream,
To keep the road both straight and right, the best I've ever seen.

9. On the eighteenth of January he sacked poor Jimmy O'Brien,
But Jimmy now has a better job than rolling on the line,
Since Lester has promoted him conductor on the tank.
To find out the conductor's name, the Honorable James O'Brien.

10. Oh, Lake Seegully is our lead down on the tree-trip road,
And when there comes a fall of snow he goes with a light load.
McQuaig he follows after him with a handsome span of grays—
Their weight is thirteen hundred, and there's stars upon the sleighs.

11. Oh, Bill Jennings, then he comes next, with Black Diamond and Gray.
The biggest load went down the road he drew the other day.

Jim Shay and Coalingham come next, their horses in good trim.
Jim Shay accuses Coalingham of jumping logs from him.

12. "Oh, that big log that you knocked down, it should have been for me.
Pat Bridgeman, he's head loader and he'll show us both fair play."
Oh, Henry Tracy, he comes next; young Hodgins is his chum.
There is John Straight and Jameson, and Tom McGuire is fun.

13. There was a man from Penesaw makes up the chosen crew.
There is one gang we have left out, we did not like to choose,
For down on the whole tree-trip road their horses are too small,
And Lake Seegully is their lead, and we don't like him at all.

14. Pat Bridgeman and Joe Merchant, they are inclined to push.
Bob Kendrick and some others, they are always in the bush.
Now here's to all the jolly boys included in our song—
And Jackson with his Percheron grays, he brings the tail along.

"The Squire Boys" again is typical of the many songs composed to describe the experiences of a particular gang, with the difficulties faced by the teamsters providing the major action.

TUNE RELATIVES. See Song 49.

23. Fine Times in Camp Number Three

Sung by LaRena Clark
Ottawa, Ontario August 1965

1. Oh, come all you young fellows and I'll sing you a song.
   It's only two verses and it won't take too long.
   It's all about lumberjacks, you plainly see,
   And the winters we spent in Camp Number Three.

REFRAIN

We had fine times in Camp Number Three.

2. Oh, the first of all was our jolly old cook.
   He kept regular hours, and he'd call us to chuck,
   And then you would hear him in the dead of the night—
   You would hear him and he'd holler that it's almost daylight!

3. Oh, the butcher he'd cheat on the weight of the meat,
   And so would the baker on the bread that we'd eat.

They would tip up the scales, and they'd lower them down,
Say we had good weight when we'd lack half a pound.

4. Oh, the next was our sawyers, and they'd make a saw bind.
Their electric light concentrate you could not find.
They would grind up their axes, to the bush they would go,
And to see them clean up boughs, it was a grand show.

5. Oh, there was a big team they named Paddy and Queen,
And it hauled the best loads that you ever had seen.
They would pile and they'd load the load ever so high—
If the harness stood pat he would load them or die.

6. Oh, there were two big teams—they drove four in a row.
As a usual thing he got stuck every load,
And then you would hear him swear loud as could be:
"Get up there in the traces, or it's crow bait you'll be!"

7. Oh, we had an old blacksmith, and you all know him well.
He would burn all the coal on the side of the hill.
He would burn all the coke and likewise the charcoal,
And his hooks would not catch in a thing he could hold.

8. Oh, here's to our foreman, and a very fine man,
And he tried to get out all the logs cut by hand.
But he never got rich, and I'll tell you the cause:
'Twas he went much too often to visit the squaws.

9. Oh, we had a young scaler, and you all know him well—
He got stuck on himself like a dizzy young swell.
He got stuck on himself while he scaled a big log,
And he could not tell punk from the end of a hog.

10. So it's now to conclude and not make it too long,
I hope I have said and done nothing that's wrong,
For my name it is Watson as you plainly see,
And I drove three big horses for Duncan and Dee.

This more unusual lumbercamp song was obviously patterned on the familiar complaint about "Hard Times" that has been sung in many parts of the continent, usually with some local adaptation. The original

British form condemned such general types as the butcher, the miller, the landlord, and the doctor, but this song deals with the particular characters in the camp and wanders off into the usual type of "moniker" song. The reference to Camp Number Three recalls the practice of carrying on lumbering operations in a single area from three or four separate camps, designated by number. The tune belongs to the familiar family of "Villikens and His Dinah."

References

"Hard Times": see Archie Green's note on "Cotton Mill Blues" in the booklet for Folkways FH 5273.

Tune Relatives

Barry, 57. Hugill, 421, 462, 466, 469. Joyce, *OIFM*, no. 526. Peacock, 123. Wilson, no. 20.

24. The Lake of the Caogama

Sung by Lennox Gavan
Quyon, Quebec   November 1964

1. Oh, now we're leaving home, me boys; to Ottawa we're goin',
   Expecting to get hired, and yet we do not know.
   We met with old Tom Patterson, saying, "Ain't you goin' awa?"
   "I'm going up the Gatineau River round the lake of the Caogama."

2. Oh, now we're leaving Ottawa in sorrow, grief, and woe;
   We're going to a place, to a place we do not know.
   We've fifty miles to travel and hard biscuits for to chaw—
   May the devil take old Patterson and the lake of the Caogama!

3. Oh, now we're in the shanty, no comfort can we find.
   We're thinking of our own dear girls, the ones we left behind,
   And dreamed that night they visit us, and their merry face we saw
   Until we woke broken-hearted round the lake of Caogama.

4. Oh, we'll all be down in April—that's if we are alive,
If Paddy doesn't keep us on the cursed creeks to drive.
There's big lakes and small lakes and lakes you never saw,
But the darndest lake among them is the lake of the Caogama.

This little song comes from the lumberwoods on the Quebec side of the Ottawa River. Lake Caogama (pronounced "Kegama") lies about eighty miles north of Arnprior. Patrick Joyce noted the old Irish tune in 1853 and set his verses about "The Leprehaun" to it.

Tune Relatives

Joyce, *AIM*, 100–101 (reprinted in Hughes III, 1–4). Hughes IV, 20–22. Ives, *NEF* 5 (1963), 72–73. O'Neill, no. 252. Petrie, no. 463. Prestige/Irish 35001 (II–7).

25. Old Holly, Crab, and I

Sung by Ron Sisson
West Guilford, Ontario October 1964

1. We work for Hay and Company; we try to do what's right.
   We start at six in the morning and quit at six at night.
   We're dumping logs upon the bay, old Holly, Crab, and I.
   The water it keeps comin' up, and we are never dry.

2. We have a shack to stay in while we wait on a load—
   It's good and handy to our work and also to the road.
   The truckers stop to see us and have a cup of tea.
   We're happy here together, old Holly, Crab, and me.

3. Some days we're not so busy so we lay on our back.
   We watch for all the trucks to come through a knothole in the shack,
   And if the firewood's getting low, we cut another tree.
   We do our best to get along, old Holly, Crab, and me.

4. Some days the loaders bull us—they really shove her through
Until we get so far behind we don't know what to do.
Especially when old Zap's around to see what he can see,
They really push it down to us, old Holly, Crab, and me.

5. Now when we've done a good day's work we put our tools away.
We're headed for the bunkhouse or wherever we may stay,
And when we've had our supper we're happy as can be.
We fool around till bedtime, old Holly, Crab, and me.

The singer, Ron Sisson, composed this comparatively recent song in 1939, when he was working for Hay and Company, a leading Haliburton lumber firm. His job was to dump the logs into the bay after the teamsters had hauled them from the bush; then they were floated to the mill to be turned into lumber.

The tune, of popular rather than folk origin, shows some resemblance to "Twinkle, Twinkle, Little Star" and is related to "The Long Peg and Awl" as sung by Tom Brandon (Jackson, p. 50).

26. We Work for Hay and Company

(To the tune of "The Wabash Cannonball.")

Sung by Ron Sisson
West Guilford, Ontario October 1964

1. We work for Hay and Company, we do the best we can.
I'll tell you what our jobs are, each and every man.
First there is Bob Barry, a likeable little cuss
Who's been working on the ladder—it's sure an awful muss!

2. The logs come up to Pompey, he sorts out the veneer.
We couldn't get along at all if Pompey wasn't here.
Now if the logs don't look so good and the bark begins to peel,
He sends them on at once to Keith, who throws the crooked steel.

3. Keith rolls them on the carriage, which is rode by Bud and Spike.
They sometimes get to fooling, which our sawyer doesn't like.
Kaufman's at the lever that runs the carriage to and fro,
And if we're cutting softwood he sure does let her go.

4. Orval tails the big saw—at this he isn't bad—
And Johnny Scott's our edgerman, the best that's to be had.
Wayne Griffen tails the edger, and he does the best he can,
Puts lumber on the trimmers, and the rest goes down to Mann.

5. There's Reggie, Mann, and Brian, they are our slab-saw crew,
And when we're cutting hardwood they haven't much to do.
H. L. Sisson is our scaler, and him you cannot fool
For he keeps one eye upon his book, the other on his rule.

6. When the boards come off the trimmers, to the boardway they must go,
And they are slowly put there by L. B. Scott, you know.
There's Calvin, Spazz, and Gerry piling lumber in the yard,
And when we're cutting hemlock, that's the only time it's hard.

7. Bill Barry is our millwright: he keeps things oiled well.
He files the saws and fixes flaws—he's busier than the rest.

Charlie Schell's the engineer—at this he can't be beat.
He keeps his engine oiled and his floors so nice and neat.

8. Stackhouse is the mill boss; he's rugged, big, and rough.
He sees we do our jobs O.K. and he helps us when it's tough.
Charlie Purdy is the foreman, but mighty right at that.
He walks around and watches things: to him we lift our hat.

9. Wibb and Jimmy are the carpenters—they know their trade quite well,
And anything they can't repair they let it go to hell.
Corby is the spare man—he has a level head.
He does the other fellows' jobs when they are sick in bed.

10. There's Lorne, our goodly office boy who keeps our time each day,
And it is certainly not his fault if we are short of pay.
Lorne is the company cook, and Norma the cookette—
She's been tagging a certain boy but hasn't caught him yet.

11. Chessel is our chore boy—he keeps the bunkhouse clean,
Plus all the other little jobs there are to be seen.
There's Hamacher and Calcin, darn fine guys are they,
The only thing about them is you can't believe what they say.

12. Me, I draw out the sawdust—I have a lot to do.
I start at five in the morning, and it's six before I'm through.
I guess this covers most of us, and you can plainly see
How we all do a good day's work for Hay and Company.

Set to the tune of "The Wabash Cannonball," this second song by Ron Sisson names each of the men who worked in Hay and Company's Redstone Mill and describes what they do. It belongs to the same genre as the "moniker" songs of the lumbercamps and, like them, gives an accurate account of the work processes. A somewhat similar Newfoundland song, "The Boys at Ninety-Five," was also set to a version of "The Wabash Cannonball" (Peacock, p. 746).

DEATH IN THE WOODS

27. The Jam on Gerry's Rocks (C 1)

A
Sung by Martin Sullivan
Nassau, Ontario June 1957

1. You shantyboys, you drivers, come list while I relate
   Concerning a young riverman and his untimely fate,
   Concerning a young riverman so manly, true, and brave—
   It was on the jam on Gerry's rocks that he met his watery grave.

2. It was on a Sunday morning as quick as you will hear.
   Our saw logs piled up mountains high, we could not keep them clear,
   Till our foreman said, "Turn out, brave boys, with hearts we'll avoid all fear.

We'll break the jam on Gerry's rocks and for Eganstown we'll steer."

3. Some of them went willingly, while others they hung back,
For to break a jam on Sunday they did not think it right,
Till six of our Canadian boys did volunteer to go
For to break the jam on Gerry's rocks with their foreman, young Monroe.

4. They had not rolled off many logs when they heard the clear voice say:
"I'd have you boys be on your guard, this jam will soon give way."
Those words were scarcely spoken when the jam did break and go
And carried off those six brave youths and their foreman, young Monroe.

5. The rest of those shantyboys those sad tidings came to hear,
In search of the drownded bodies down the river they did steer,
Till one of those poor bodies to their sad grief and woe
All bruised and mangled by the rocks lay the head of young Monroe.

6. They raised him from his watery grave, combed back his coal black hair.
There was one fair form amongst them whose cries would rend the air:
There was one fair form amongst them, a girl from Saginaw town;
Her moans and cries would rend the skies for her true love that was drowned.

7. Poor Clara did not survive long through her sad grief and woe.
. . . .
It was in about three weeks after that she was called to go,
And her last request was granted, to be laid by young Monroe.

8. So come all of you bold shantyboys, I'd have you call and see
A little mound by the river bend where stands a hemlock tree,
And the shantyboys cut the woods all down, two lovers there lie low:
There lies Miss Clara Verner and her true love, young Monroe.

B

Sung by O. J. Abbott
Hull, Quebec   August 1957

1. Oh, come all you jolly shantyboys wherever that you be,
I hope you'll pay attention and listen unto me
Concerning six young shantyboys so manly and so brave:
It was at the jam on Gerry's rocks they met with a watery grave.

2. It was on a Sunday morning as you shall quickly hear.
Our logs they piled up mountains high, we could not keep them clear.
Our boss he says, "Turn out, my boys, with hearts full of good cheer.
We'll break the jam on Gerry's rocks and for Egantown we'll steer."

3. Oh, some of them were willing, while more they did stand back:
To work upon the Sunday they did not think it right.
But six Canadian shantyboys did volunteer and go
To break the jam on Gerry's rocks with their foreman, young Monroe.

4. They had not rolled off many logs when the boss to them did say:
"I would have you to be on your guard; this jam will soon give way."
He had scarcely spoken those few words when the jam did break and go,
And carried off those six bold youths with their foreman, young Monroe.

5. When the rest of those young shantyboys those tidings came to hear,
To search for their dead comrades to the river they did steer.
There found a lifeless body to their sad grief and woe,
All cut and mangled on the beach was the head of young Monroe.

6. They raised it from the water, combed down the wavy hair.
There was one fair form amongst them, her cries would rend the air.

There was one fair form amongst them, a girl from Saginaw town.
Her moans and cries would rend the skies for her true love that was drowned.

7. Miss Clara was a noble girl, likewise a raftsman's friend.
Her mother was a widow lived by the river's bend.
The wages of her own true love the boss to her did pay,
And a liberal subscription she received from the shantyboys next day.

8. They gave him a decent burial, it being on the sixth of May.
Let the rest of ye young shantyboys for your dead comrades pray.
In less than three weeks after, this maid was called to go,
And her last request was that she might be buried with young Monroe.

9. On a little mound by the riverside there grows a hemlock tree:
The name, the date, and drowning of our hero you may see.
The shantyboys cut the woods all round, two lovers here lie low:
Here lies Miss Clara Fenton and her lover, *young Monroe.*

This most widespread of all shanty songs is found not only in every northeastern collection but as far afield as Florida, Oklahoma, Oregon, and Scotland. In Ontario, as elsewhere, it is by far the best-known lumbering ballad.

Fannie Eckstorm, who has studied it most thoroughly, says that it has two forms, an early and a late one, and that "The old form of the song is readily distinguishable by the variable name of the heroine and by finding the head, not the body, of young Monroe on the river-bank." The old form also mentions the six shantyboys in the first stanza, whereas the later one focuses on young Monroe. O. J. Abbott's version follows the old pattern throughout and is remarkably close to Fannie Eckstorm's *C* text. Martin Sullivan's falls between the two forms, retaining "the head of young Monroe" but approximating the standard name of "Clara Vernon." Other Ontario versions, like the one sung by Tom Brandon on Folkways FM 4052, follow the late pattern.

The Ontario tunes all belong to the common strain that Barry,

Rickaby, and Doerflinger give for this song, Martin Sullivan's being unusually tuneful and having a rather daring rhythmic flux. Elsewhere the tune used is one found in Ontario for "Peter Emery" and "The Farmer's Son and the Shantyboy."

References

PRINTED. Laws, *NAB*, 147. Dorson, *Buying the Wind*, 103–105, and *FFMA* 8: 1 (1966), 13–18. Gard, 64. Grover, 181–182. Greenleaf, 331–332. Holbrook, 131–133. Korson, 345–346. Leach, 256–257. Mackenzie, 367–370. Manny, 115–117. Moore, 341–343. Peacock, 752–753. Vincent, 2–3.

RECORDED. Folk Legacy FSC 9 (Hare). Folkways FM 4001 (Warde Ford), FM 4052 (Brandon), FW 6821 (Hemsworth). Library of Congress AAFS L56 (Bill McBride, Jim Kirkpatrick). *Checklist*, 105–106 ("Foreman Monroe"), 192. National Museum FO 20-185 (Abbott), FO 20-186 (Sullivan).

Tune Relatives

Barry, 52, 56. Bayard, 9. E. C. Beck, *Lore*, 195. Colcord, 126. Creighton, *MFS*, 195, 202. Creighton and Senior, 267. Doerflinger, 238, 239, 241, 243. Flanders *et al.*, 44. Galvin, 65. Gardner, 278. Grainger, nos. 274, 275, 276, 277. Leach, 256. Manny, 220, 241, 272. O'Lochlainn, 44. Peacock, 375, 518, 775. Petrie, nos. 26, 48, 185, 328, 329. Rickaby, 11, 15, 18, 19. Sandburg, 394.

28. Johnny Murphy (C 2)

Sung by John Leahy
Douro, Ontario November 1958

1. One evening last June as I rambled
   All over the hills and valleys alone,
   The mosquitee notes was melodious;
   How merry the whippoorwill sang!
   The frogs in the marshes was croaking,
   And the tree toads were whistling for rain,
   And the partridge around me were drumming
   On the banks of the Little L'Eau Pleine.

2. As the sun to the west was declining
It tainted the tree tops with red.
My wandering steps bore me onward,
Never caring where'er they had led,
Till I chanced for to meet a young school ma'am,
Charmed in a horrible strain.
She lamented her lost jolly raftsman
From the banks of the Little L'Eau Pleine.

3. "Pray tell me what kind of a fellow
And what kind of clothing he wore,
For I did belong to that river
And I might have seen him somewhere."
"His pants they were made of two wheat sacks
With a patch a foot square on each knee.
His jacket and shirt they were dyed with
The bark of a butternut tree.

4. "He wore a red sash round his middle
And an end hanging down on each side.
His boots numbered ten of strong cowhide
And the heels about four inches wide.
His name it was Honest John Murphy,
And on it there ne'er was a stain,
For he loved the West Constant River—
That's the reason he left the L'Eau Pleine."

5. "If that be the kind of your Johnny,
'Twas him I did know well.
The sad tiding I'll tell you,
Your Johnny was drowned in the dell.
We buried him 'neath the low valley,
And you ne'er shall behold him again,
For the stone marks the sod o'er your Johnny.
He lies far from the Little L'Eau Pleine."

6. When she heard the sad tidings she fainted;
She fell to the ground as if dead.
I scooped up my hat full of water,

And I poured it all over her head.
She opened her eyes and looked wildly:
I thought she was nearly insane.
I thought to myself, "She'll go crazy
On the banks of the Little L'Eau Pleine."

7. "Now I'll desert my location
And not teach district schools any more.
I'll go where I'll never, no never,
Hear the sound of a fifty-foot oar.
I'll go to some far distant island,
To England, to Ireland, or Spain,
But I'll never forget Johnny Murphy
On the banks of the Little L'Eau Pleine."

As Rickaby notes, W. N. Allen composed "The Banks of the Little Eau Pleine" in the 1870's, using the pattern of "The Lass of Dunmore." The Little Eau Pleine is a small tributary of the Wisconsin River near Stevens Point. This ballad, the most popular of various songs Mr. Allen wrote under the pseudonym of Shan T. Boy, passed into tradition in Wisconsin, Michigan, Minnesota, and Ontario and spread eastward to New Brunswick and Prince Edward Island.

The song is not common in Ontario: John Leahy is the only one who has sung it for me, although Lorne Gardiner says that Reuben Beilhartz knows it as "The Little Oak Plain." Mr. Leahy sings it as "the little low plain" and changes the Wisconsin River to the "West Constant." The thirteen somewhat discursive stanzas of the original have been whittled down to seven, but these still tell the full story. Most of the semihumorous details that marked Mr. Allen's verses have disappeared, except for the "hat full of water."

The tune, used also in Rickaby's versions, derives from "The Green Mossy Banks of the Lea," but it forms a distinct strain. It is commonly used for "Erin's Green Shore" and turns up in two fine Newfoundland songs, "The Blooming Bright Star of Belle Isle" and "The Green Shores of Fogo." Mr. Leahy's version has an unusual regular shifting of meter, which fluctuates betwen 6/8 and 4/8.

REFERENCES

PRINTED. Laws, *NAB*, 147–148. Gard, 101–104. Gordon MSS, 419. Manny, 215–217. Ives, *NEF* 5 (1963), 48–52.

RECORDED. Folkways FM 4052 (Leahy).

TUNE RELATIVES

Barry, 54. E. C. Beck, *Lore*, 151. Creighton, *MFS*, 165; *SBNS*, 167. Fowke, 88–89 (and Prestige/International 25014, I–1). Greenleaf, 268. Hughes, II, 60–63, IV, 6–7. Mackenzie, 397. Manny, 268. Ives, *NEF* 5 (1963), 49–50, 78 n. O'Lochlainn, 114. O'Neill, nos. 102, 103, 486. Peacock, 362, 522, 598. Petrie, no. 1254. Rickaby, 30, 34. Sandburg, 40. Wilson, 28 (no. 22).

29. Jimmy Judge (C 4)

A

Sung by George McCallum
Grafton, Ontario March 1961

1. Jimmy Judge was this young man's name, I'm going to let you know,
   And I mean to sing his praises wherever I do go,
   For he was as fine a young man as ever the sun shone on,
   And 'twas on that Bonneshai River that he was drownded on.

2. His parents searched the Bonneshai his most precious corpse to find.
   While a fisherman while a-fishing was, a watery corpse he spied.
   He was as fine a young man as ever the sun shone on,
   And 'twas on that Bonneshai River that he was drownded on.

B

Sung by Jim Brown
Marlbank, Ontario November 1960

1. Come all you wild heroes that runs the restless deep,

Just think of the sad fate of him who now beneath you sleep.
It was of as fine a young man as ever the sun shined on,
Down on those foaming waters he found a dismal doom.

2. It was on the Bonneshai River aways below Renfrew
That he went for to break the jam and with it he went through.
In spite of his activity his precious life to save,
In vain was his exertion; he found a watery grave.

3. It was early the next morning the raftsmen all did join.
They all sailed out together this young man for to find.
They searched the deep in every place where the current does swiftly fly,
'Twas a fisher boy, as I am told, his floating corpse did spy.

4. It would melt your heart with pity when they brought him on the shore
For to see his handsome features with the rocks all cut and tore,
To see so fine a young man all in his youthful bloom.
Down on these foaming waters he found a dismal doom.

5. Oh, the lass that loved him dearly, she cries, "Now I'm undone."
Likewise his agéd parents, they cries, "My darlin' son."
But now he is in Paradise and happy he may be,
For I hope in heaven his soul will shine for all eternity.

Though this account of an Ontario tragedy spread far afield, it has not been well preserved. It has been collected in Michigan, Maine, and New York, but most texts are defective and the names corrupted. The earliest text, which Barry printed in the *Bulletin of the Folksong Society of the Northeast* (No. 10, p. 20), is more complete and coherent than later versions.

Of the Ontario versions, Jim Brown's is the most complete, but George McCallum's indicates the fragmentation that usually occurs. Joe Thibadeau sang a slightly longer but more disjointed version. All Ontario singers call the hero "Jimmy Judge" and all mention the "Bonneshai River"—actually the Bonnechère that flows into the Ottawa east of Renfrew. Barry's version has a tune derived from "The Jam on Gerry's Rocks," but all the Ontario singers use a different tune, one with a distinctly Irish cast and found both in Ireland and North America for many different songs.

The Reverend Joseph E. Gravelle says that James Angus Judge was born at Chapeau, Quebec, in 1846, the youngest of the three sons of Dr. John J. Judge, born in Ireland in 1813. Dr. Judge was Eganville's first medical practitioner, and he later moved to Aylmer, Quebec, just west of Hull. Father Gravelle believes that the drowning took place in about 1866, when Jimmy was twenty years old.

References

PRINTED. Laws, *NAB*, 149. Fowke and Johnston, 80–81. Warner, 73. Gravelle, *Renfrew Advance*, September 29, 1966 (texts same as above).

RECORDED. National Museum FO 20-187 (Brown); FO 20-188 (McCallum).

Tune Relatives

Bayard, 11. Broadwood, 68, 102. Cazden, *Abelard* I, 24–25, 107–108 n. Colcord, 173. Creighton, *MFS*, 6, 19, 71, 103, 166. Edwards, 126. Hughes II, 70–75; IV, 8–13, 34–38. Hugill, 411, 412. Ives, *Larry Gorman*, 33–34. Joyce, *OIFM*, nos. 92, 133, 158, 393, 404, 405, 415. Leach, 242. O'Lochlainn, 184. O'Neill, nos. 96, 164, 242, 396, 397, 428, 473, 580. Peacock, 640, 755, 875 (second half of tune), 854 (complete tune). Petrie, nos. 37, 75, 193, 202, 252, 322, 323, 469, 648, 863, 1069, 1340. Sharp I, 200; II, 79.

30. Johnny Stiles (C 5)

A

Sung by Emerson Woodcock
Peterborough, Ontario July 1957

1. Come all you wild boys from the river,
   Come listen to me for awhile,
   And I will relate you a story
   Of a chum and kind friend, Johnny Stiles.

2. 'Twas away by the wild Moose River,
   Away down by the old Dimee Dam,
   One morning while eating our breakfast,
   On the rock there we saw a big jam.

3. We scarcely had finished our breakfast,
   Straightway we did go to the jam,
   While some of our boys took the pole trail
   For the flood from the reservoir dam.

4. We drove her down to the deep water,
   Our peavies and pikes we applied,
   Little dreaming that one of our number
   That day would so horribly die.

5. We drove her down to the deep water—
   Our foreman he shouts, we obey.
   Not one of our boys but had drove her;
   Not one of our boys were afraid.

6. On the river there never was better,
   As I said, my young friend, Johnny Stiles.
   He had drove her far oftener than any,
   But he always seemed careless and wild.

7. Bad luck seemed against him this morning,
   For his foot it got caught in a jam,
   And you know how those waters go howling
   In a flood from the reservoir dam.

8. We were there in less than a moment
   From the time he gave his first shout,
   But you know when those waters go howling,
   They roll in but they never roll out.

9. We drove her down to the deep water
   While the sweat from our foreheads did pour,
   And we pulled his dead body from under,
   But it looked like poor Johnny no more.

10. For his flesh it hung down in large ringlets,
    In pieces the size of your hand.
    On earth we found rest for his body,
    May the Lord keep his soul in command.

B "Johnny Doyle"
Sung by Bill Hughey
Peterborough, Ontario March 1957

1. Come all you wild boys of the river,
   Just listen to me for awhile.
   I will relate you a story
   Of a friend and kind chum, Johnny Doyle.

2. Up on the wild Moose River
   By the side of the big Jumbo Dam

One morning while eating our breakfast
We spied on the rocks a big jam.

3. Shortly after breakfast was over
Our peavies and pikes made a way,
Some of the boys took the pole trail,
Not one of us knew no delay.

4. On the river there never was better
Than my friend as I say Johnny Doyle.
He's driven it oftener than any
But always was reckless and wild.

5. But this morning his luck went against him,
His foot it got caught in the jam,
And you know how that water keeps howling
From the falls at the reservoir dam.

6. We obeyed the command of our foreman
Till the sweat in our face it did pour.
We took his body from under,
But it looked like poor Johnny no more.

7. His flesh it was cut into ringlets,
Not a piece left the size of your hand.
On earth his body lies resting,
And the Lord has his soul in command.

Of all the tragic lumbering ballads, this ranks second only to "The Jam on Gerry's Rocks" among Ontario singers. It is known here both as "Johnny Doyle" and "Johnny Stiles," but the site is always "the wild Moose River," though American singers usually name "the wild Mustard River." "Johnny Doyle" was probably the original; it would be corrupted to "Stiles" by the Irish habit of pronouncing "Doyle" as "D'yle." Because of its popularity in Ontario, I believe it tells of a tragedy here, but I have not been able to pin it down.

Joe Kelly sings another version of "Johnny Doyle," and Tom Brandon, George McCallum, and Joe Thibadeau know it as "Johnny Stiles." All except Joe Thibadeau sing it to much the same tune, which seems to be derived from the first part of "Rosin the Beau."

References

PRINTED. Laws, *NAB*, 149. Manny, 306–307.

RECORDED. Folkways FM 4052 (Kelly, Brandon). Library of Congress AAFS L56 (Carl Lathrop). National Museum FO 4-35 (Hughey), FO 4-36 (Woodcock), FO 20-194 (McCallum).

Tune Relatives

E. C. Beck, *Lore*, 202–203. Brown V, 32–34. Fowke and Mills, 178. Greenleaf, 324. Kidson, 94. Manny, 76, 306. Peacock, 418, 748. Petrie, no. 1541. Wilson, 21 (no. 9), 43 n.

31. Jimmy Whelan (C 7)

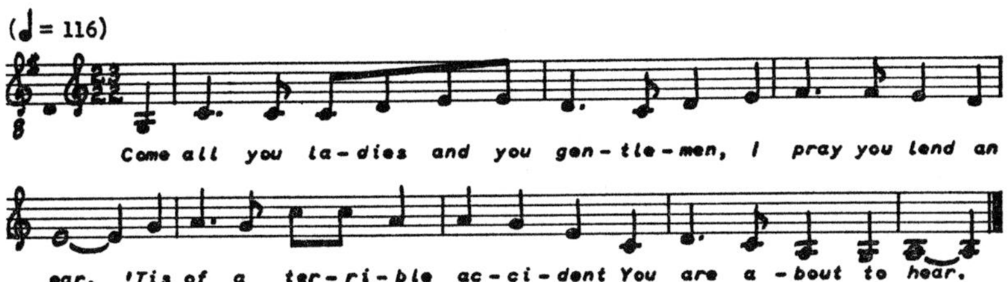

Sung by Emerson Woodcock
Peterborough, Ontario September 1957

1. Come all you ladies and you gentlemen,
   I pray you lend an ear.
   'Tis of a terrible accident
   You are about to hear.

2. Tis of a young and active youth,
   Jimmy Whelan he was called;
   He was drownded on McClellan's drive
   All on the Upper Falls.

3. The fierce and the raging main,
   The waters they ran high,
   And the foreman said to Whelan:
   "This jam you will have to try.

4. "You've always been an active youth
   While danger's lurking near,
   So you are the man I want to help
   To keep those waters clear."

5. Whelan he made answer
   Unto his comrades bold:
   "Supposing if there's danger,
   We will do as we are told.

6. "We'll obey our foreman's orders
   As noble men should do"—

Just as he spoke the jam it broke
And let poor Whelan through.

7. The raging main it tossed and tore
Those logs from shore to shore,
And here and there his body went,
A-tumbling o'er and o'er.

8. No earthly man could ever live
In such a raging main.
Poor Whelan struggled hard for life
But he struggled all in vain.

9. There were three of them in danger,
But two of them were saved.
It was noble-hearted Whelan
That met with a watery grave.

10. So come all you young and active youths,
A warning from me take,
And try to shun all danger
Before it gets too late,

11. For death is drawing nearerer
And trying to destroy
The pride of some poor mother's heart
And his father's only joy.

Unlike Johnny Doyle's, the time and place of Jimmy Whelan's death are known. As Rickaby notes, the hero's real name was James Phalen, and he was killed in 1878 on Ontario's Mississippi River, a tributary of the Ottawa. The tragedy occurred when two rafts of logs coming out of Cross Lake collided in the swift waters of King's Chute. As the raftsmen worked to untangle the jam, Phalen slipped off a shifting log and was pulled under by the current. The McClellan mentioned was Peter McLaren, an Ottawa lumberman who made a fortune and became a Canadian senator before he died in 1919.

James Phalen's grandniece, Miss Mary C. Phalen of Ottawa, thinks the drowning took place in the spring of 1876 rather than 1878. She says that the composer of the song was believed to be Timothy Doyle, son of a pioneer farmer in Drummond Township.

The ballad spread to Michigan, Wisconsin, Minnesota, Maine, Pennsylvania, and New Brunswick, but, although it became more widely known than either "Johnny Doyle" or "Jimmy Judge," it is not now as well remembered in Ontario. Emerson Woodcock is the only singer I found who knows it. His tune, different from the families noted by Barry, Rickaby, and Doerflinger, is very close to "Auld Lang Syne."

The number of rivermen who died in accidents like the one detailed here will never be known. Mr. Arlington Fraser of Lancaster quoted a former shantyboy, Ray Ciegle, who told him that there were twenty-seven crosses beside one rapid near Pembroke.

References

PRINTED. Laws, *NAB*, 150. Fowke, 124–125 (same as above). Shoemaker, 86–88. Vincent, 39–40.

RECORDED. Folkways FM 4052 (Woodcock).

Tune Relatives

Fowke, 42, 48 (and Folkways FM 4051, II–8).

32. Lost Jimmy Whelan (C 8)

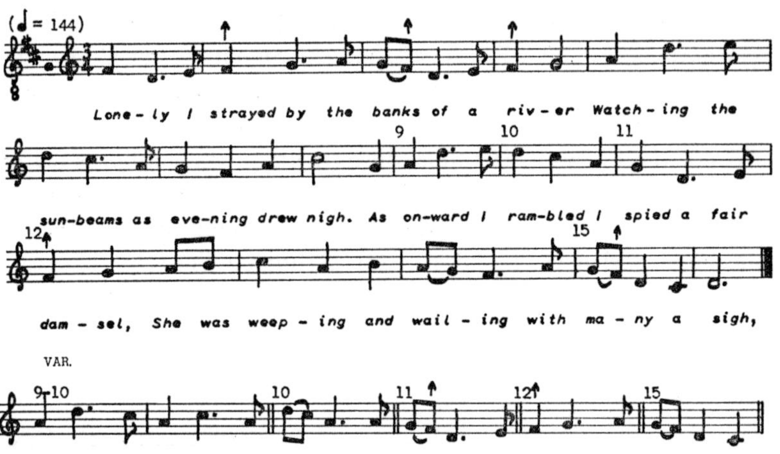

Sung by Martin Sullivan
Nassau, Ontario June 1957

1. Lonely I strayed by the banks of a river
Watching the sunbeams as evening drew nigh.
As onward I rambled I spied a fair damsel,
She was weeping and wailing with many a sigh,

2. Crying for one who is now lying lonely,
Sighing for one who no mortal could see,
For the dark rolling waters flow gently around him
As onward she speeds over young Jimmy's grave.

3. She cries, "Oh, my darling, won't you come to my arrums
And give me fond kisses which ofttimes you gave?
You promised to meet me this evening, my darling,
So now, lovelie Jimmy, arise from your grave."

4. Slowly he rose from the dark stormy waters,
A vision of beauty far fairer than sun.
Pink and red were the garments all round him,
And unto this fair maid to speak he began,

5. Saying, "Why do you rise me from the re-alms of glory
Back to this place where I once had to leave?"
"It was to embrace in your strong loving arrums,
So now lovelie Jimmy, take me to your grave."

6. "Darling," he says, "you are asking a favor
That no earthly mortal could grant unto thee,
For death is the debtor that tore us asunder
And wide is the gulf, love, between you and me.

7. "Hard, hard were the struggles on the cruel Mississippi,
But encircled around her on every side,
Thinking of you as we conquered them bravely,
I was hoping some day for to make you my bride.

8. "But in vain was the hopes that arose in my bosom,
And nothing, oh nothing, on earth could be saved.
My last dying thoughts were of God and you, darling,
Till death took me down to the deep silent grave.

9. "One fond embrace, love, and then I must leave you.
One loving farewell, and then we must part."
Cold were the arms that encircled around her
And cold was the form that she pressed to her heart.

10. Slowly he rose from the banks of the river.
Up to the sky he then seemed to go,
Leaving this fair maid on the banks of the river,
Sighing and weeping in anger and woe.

11. Throwing herself on the banks of the river,
Crying as though her poor heart it would break,
She cried, "Oh, my darling, my lost Jimmy Whelan,
I'll lie down and die by the side of *your grave*."

Although this song is obviously based on an older British ballad, the original has not been identified. A close relative is the Scottish "Blantyre Explosion," which describes a disaster near Glasgow in 1877. It uses the same tune, and its first two stanzas are very similar, even to the line "A-weeping and wailing with many a sigh." Like

"Lost Jimmy Whelan," it seems to be an adaptation of an older ballad to fit a local tragedy.

"Lost Jimmy Whelan" is more common in Ontario than "Jimmy Whelan," and it is also well known in Nova Scotia and Newfoundland. Though all versions mention the hero's death by drowning, only one other, a six-stanza text from Michigan, specifically links it to the accident on "the cruel Mississippi." Martin Sullivan's text is one of the most complete that has been reported, and his tune is one commonly used for "The Lass of Glenshee," also popular in Ontario.

References

PRINTED. Laws, *NAB*, 150–151. Fowke and Johnston, 77–79 (same as above). Lomax and Lomax, *American Ballads*, 445–446 (reprinted from Rickaby, 24). Manny, 263–264. Peacock, 385–389.

RECORDED. Folkways FM 4001 (Robert Walker), FE 4075 (Mary Dumphy). National Museum FO 4-37 (Dave McMahon), FO 4-38 (O. J. Abbott), FO 4-39 (Sullivan).

Tune Relatives

Barry, 12. Cazden, *Abelard* I, 92. Creighton, *MFS*, 72, 114, 115. Creighton and Senior, 186. Fowke, 132. Leach, 98, 210. Lloyd, 129. Manny, 263. Peacock, 385, 387. Folkways FM 4051 (I–6).

33. Harry Bale (C 13)

A

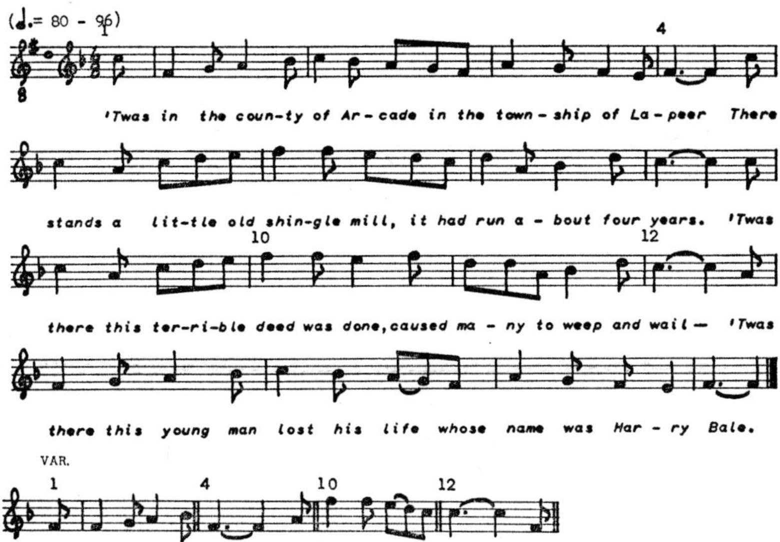

Sung by Minnie Molloy
Coehill, Ontario August 1957

1. 'Twas in the county of Arcade in the township of Lapeer
   There stands a little old shingle mill, it had run about four years.
   'Twas there this terrible deed was done, caused many to weep and wail—
   'Twas there this young man lost his life whose name was Harry Bale.

2. By lowering down to lift the shaft which threw the carriage in gear
   It threw him up against the saw and cut him so severe.
   It cut him through the shoulder blade and halfway down the back;
   It threw him out upon the floor as the carriage it ran back.

3. His brothers they were sent for, likewise his sisters too.
   The doctors came to dress the wounds, alas, it was too true.
   And when the fatal wounds were dressed he unto them did say:
   "I guess there is no hope for me and I soon shall pass away . . ."

B "Harry Dale"

Sung by Emerson Woodcock
Peterborough, Ontario August 1957

1. Kind friends and tender parents, come listen to my song,
   And if you but attention pay I'll not detain you long,
   For it's of a poor unfortunate lad who is known both far and near—
   His parents raised him tenderly not many miles from here.

2. 'Twas in the county of Rockin in the township of Apeer,
   There stands a little shingle mill, which ran about one year.

'Twas there this awful deed was done caused many to weep and wail—
'Twas there this young man lost his life whose name was Harry Dale.

3. It seemed his occupation was a sawyer in a mill,
For he followed it successfully one year, three months, until
It came his turn to leave this world, this world of grief and care.
God knows how soon it will be our turn to follow him up there.

4. On the twenty-fourth day of April in the year of seventy-nine
He went to work as usual, no trouble did he resign.
At the lowering of the feedboard threw his carriage into gear,
Which ran him up against the saw and cut him so severe.

5. It cut him through the shoulder blade and halfway down the back
And threw him out upon the floor—the carriage it came back.
He started for the shanty—his strength it failed him fast.
Said he, "My boys, I'm wounded and I fear it is my last."

6. A doctor then was sent for, likewise his sisters too.
When the doctor came to dress his wounds, alas, it was too true,
And when his fatal wounds were dressed, he unto them did say:
"I know there is no hopes for me and I soon shall pass away."

7. Poor Harry had no father to watch beside his bed,
Nor a kind and gentle mother to soothe his aching head.
He lingered on both day and night till death did ease his pain.
Hushed was his voice forever, and he never shall speak again.

8. They put him in his coffin and fitted him for his grave,
And now his buddies do mourn for him, for the loss of a brother so brave.
They carried him to the churchyard, laid his body down to rest,
And now his body lies moldering *and his spirit is with the blest.*

As Gardner and Beck note, nineteen-year-old Harry Bahel was killed on April 29, 1879, in Arcadia Township, Lapeer County, Michigan. Both Harry's brother Charles and a friend, Johnny Coffee, have been credited with composing the ballad. As one would expect, it was most widely sung in Michigan, but it also spread to Arkansas, Minnesota, and Pennsylvania and was fairly popular in Ontario. Harry's name has become variously Bale, Dale, Bell, and Vale, and his township and county have suffered similar corruptions.

Emerson Woodcock sings a complete version that compares quite closely to Bill McBride's Michigan text. Minnie Molloy's is much abbreviated but still tells the whole story—an excellent example of folk condensation. Their tunes belong to different families: Mrs. Molloy's is like the one that Gardner gives for this song and that Barry has for "Samuel Allen," whereas Mr. Woodcock's is more unusual.

REFERENCES

PRINTED. Laws, *NAB*, 153. Manny, 261–262. Shoemaker, 92–93.

RECORDED. National Museum FO 20-189 (Woodcock), FO 20-190 (Molloy).

TUNE RELATIVES

A. Barry, 70. E. C. Beck, *Lore*, 219. Brown IV, 207. Cazden, *Abelard* I, 36. Creighton, *SBNS*, 328. Doyle, 9. Flanders *et al.*, 92. Galvin, 45. Gardner, 278. Hughes IV, 101–104. Ives, *NEF* 7 (1965), 41–42. Joyce, *OIFM*, no. 55. Leach, 96, 252. Mackenzie, 404. Manny, 115, 152, 261, 274, 301. O'Neill, no. 99. Peacock, 763, 765. Petrie nos. 324, 634. Thorp, 144–145. Wilson, 36–38 (no. 30, except 30g, 30l, 30n), 45–46 n. Folk Legacy FSC 10 (I–2, I–4). Prestige/International 25014 (A–11, B–8).

B. Galvin, 46. Ives, *NEF* 7 (1965), 64. Kidson, 63.

34. Harry Dunn (C 14)

A

Sung by Martin Sullivan
Nassau, Ontario June 1957

1. There's many's a poor Canadian boy leaves home and friends so dear
   And longing for excitement to Michigan did steer.
   I once knew a charming lad, his name was Harry Dunn,
   His father was a farmer in the county of Lodun.

2. He'd all the wealth he could possess and land of high estate.
   He only wanted to have a time in the woods of Michigan,
   And on the morning he left his home, his mother to him did say:
   "Now Harry dear, take my advice, and on the farm do stay.

3. "You leave your kind old mother, likewise your sisters three,
And something seems to tell me no more your face I'll see."
He went into the city, and he hired with a lumbering king;
He strayed away and took his course to the woods of Pennslavane.

4. He worked away for three long months. Ofttimes he would write home,
Saying, "The winter will soon be over, and then I will go down."
He rose one morning from his bunk, his face it wore no smile.
He called his comrade out of doors whose name was Charlie Lyle,

5. Saying, "Charlie dear, I had a dream that filled my heart with woe.
I fear there's something wrong at home, and there I'd better go."
His comrade only laughed at him, which pleased him for a time,
Saying, "Charlie dear, come let us go, it's time to fall the pine."

6. They worked away till one o'clock that very afternoon,
When a hanging limb fell down on him and sealed his fateful doom.
His comrades gathered all round him to pull the limb away,
Saying, "Charlie dear, I'm dying, and my time has come right soon.

7. "Now Charlie dear, go down with me and take my body home,
And tell my kind old mother what caused me for to roam."
His poor old agéd mother, she fell down like a stone.
They raised her up, but her heart was broke when her Harry was brought home.

8. His poor old agéd father, he lingered for a while,
But never after on this earth was ever seen to smile.
In less than three weeks after, they buried that good old man,
So then you see a deathly curse lies over Michi*gan*.

B

Sung by Nelson Lewis
Harcourt, Ontario October 1964

1. I know a lad, a charming lad, whose name was Harry Dunn.
His father was a farmer in the township of Leedun.
He had everything you could possess and a farm of good land,
But he only wanted to have a time in the woods of Michigan.

2. The morning that he went away his mother to him did say,
Saying, "Harry, dear, take my advice and on the farm do stay.
You'll leave your poor old mother, likewise your sisters three—
There's something tells me that your face no more on earth shall see."

3. The morning that he left his bunk on his face he wore no smile.
He called his comrade to the door whose name was Charlie Lyle,
Saying, "Charlie, dear, I had a dream which filled my heart with woe.
I fear there's something wrong at home, and there I'd better go."

4. His comrade only laughed at him, which pleased him for awhile,
Saying, "Harry, dear, we'd better go—'tis time to fall the pine."
They worked away till two o'clock all on that fatal day
When a hanging limb fell down on him and squashed him to the clay.

5. His comrades gathered round him to take the limb away,
Saying, "Comrades, I am dying. My time has come today.
May God in his kind mercy pity my poor friends at home
And, Charlie, you go along with me and take my body down."

6. The poor old woman she left the room, she lingered for awhile
And never known while after to ever wear a smile.
The poor old man he gazed at him, he fell down like a stone.
They picked him up, his heart being broke, it was his only son.

7. . . . .
. . . .
In less than two months after they buried the poor old man,
And now you see the deadly curse *hangs over Michigan.*

The date and place of the accident detailed here have never been established, but similar tragedies were common in the lumberwoods, where a hanging limb was known as a widow-maker.

The ballad is well known in Michigan and Ontario and fairly widespread on the east coast. Martin Sullivan's text and tune are typical, the tune being derived from "The Wild Colonial Boy." Nelson Lewis's text shows the condensation such ballads eventually undergo, and his tune, commonly associated with "The Texas Rangers," has been used for many other lumbering songs.

References

PRINTED. Laws, *NAB*, 153. E. C. Beck, *Lore*, 212–217. Peacock, 763–765. Waugh, *JAF* 31 (1918), 75.

RECORDED. Folkways FM 4052 (Sullivan). National Museum FO 4-42 (O. J. Abbott).

Tune Relatives

A. Barry, 20, 63. H. P. Beck, 98. Doyle, 42, 46. Fowke, 24 (and Folkways FM 4051, II–7). Fowke and Mills, 76, 108–109. Galvin 55. Gardner, 326. Harlow, 177. Ives, *Larry Gorman*, 46–47. Joyce, *OIFM*, nos. 298, 303. Leach, 148. Manny, 49, 126, 224, 283, 304. O'Lochlainn, 198. O'Neill, no. 411. Peacock, 562, 905, 931. Petrie, nos. 26, 48. Ranson, 56. Wilson, 16–19 (no. 5). Folkways FM 4053 (II–5).

B. Creighton, *MFS*, 150. Ives, *NEF* 7 (1965), 81–82. Jackson, 47. Lomax and Lomax, *Cowboy Songs*, 359, 361. Manny, 52, 111. Morris, 29. Randolph II, 160. Thomas, 108–109. Wilson, 24 (no. 19) and Folkways FM 4053, I–5. Prestige/International 25014 (II–3).

35. Whitney's Camp

(To the tune of Song 34A.)

Sung by Nelson Lewis
Harcourt, Ontario October 1964

1. It's of a brave young shantyboy, brave-hearted, true,
He left his home near Ottawa, and to Whitney's camp did come.
He worked away for two long months; ofttimes he would write home,
Saying, "The winter will soon be over, and then I will come down."

2. He worked away till on that fatal day
When a hanging limb fell down on him and squashed him to the clay.
They rolled him in his blanket and placed him in the sleigh
And started for Long Lake Camp 'bout twenty miles away.

This fragmentary ballad is obviously patterned on "Harry Dunn," which is natural enough for it describes another lad who died in the same kind of accident. Only the location is different: the town of Whitney is in northern Ontario between Renfrew and Huntsville, and it lies a few miles from one of Ontario's many Long Lakes.

Strangely enough, Nelson Lewis sang this ballad to the usual tune for "Harry Dunn," although he used a less typical tune for his version of "Harry Dunn."

36. Peter Emery (C 27)

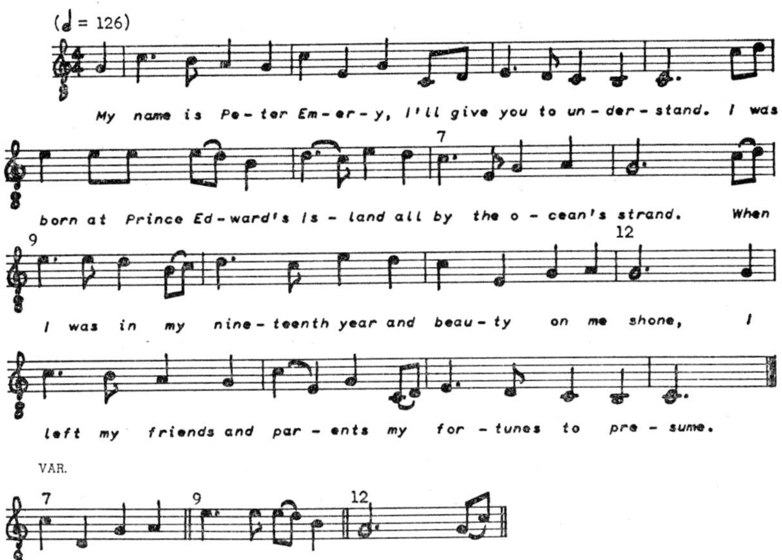

A
Sung by Martin McManus
Peterborough, Ontario June 1957

1. My name is Peter Emery, I'll give you to understand.
   I was born at Prince Edward's Island all by the ocean's strand.
   When I was in my nineteenth year and beauty on me shone,
   I left my friends and parents my fortune to presume.

2. I hired with a contract lumberman, I'll give you to understand,
   . . . .
   For to go into the lumberwoods where they cut those tall trees down.
   'Twas loading log sleighs at the skids that I met my fatal doom.

3. There's danger in the ocean, where the waves roll mountain high;
   There's danger on the battlefields, where the angry bullets fly;
   There's danger in the lumbering sheds, but death lurks seldom there
   Until I fell a victim all unto that monstrous snare.

4. Alas, my cruel father, it was he who drove me here.
   [I could not bear his treatments for they were so severe.]
   It is not right for to press a boy or to try to keep him down—
   'Twill cause him for to leave his home when he is far too young.

5. There's another that I'll speak about—it is my mother dear,
   Who raised a son so young to part as I left her tender care.
   'Twas little did poor mother think when I was but a boy
   In this country I would ramble or this death that I would die.

6. There's another that I'll speak about: that island girl so true.
   Long may she live to enjoy the spot where first my breath I drew,
   For time will roll on just the same as before I passed away.
   What signifies the death of one whose bones are only clay?

7. Here's adieu to Prince Edward's Island, a garden in the sea.
   No more I'll walk her flowery dells or smell the scented breeze,
   Or sit and watch her gallant ships as they go sailing by
   With their white flags floating in the breeze beneath the summer sky.

8. There is one more request I will ask of you, and this one I will crave:
   That my Heavenly Father will bless the spot where my moldering bones are laid.
   Far from the village of boyhood town my moldering bones are laid
   For to wait the Saviour's calling to that awful *judgment day.*

B

Sung by Joe Thibadeau
Bobcaygeon, Ontario   October 1964

1. My name is Peter Emery, as you may understand.
   I was brought up in Prince Edward's Isle close by the ocean's strand.
   In eighteen hundred and ninety-one when the flowers were in full bloom,
   I left my native country my fortune to presume.

2. I landed in New Brunswick, that lumbering counteree,
   And I hired for to work in the lumbering woods in southwest Miramichi.
   I hired for to work in the lumberwoods where they cut the tall pine down.
   While loading a sleigh at a skidway I received a fatal wound.

3. It's adieu unto my father—it was him who sent me here.
   I could not bear his treatments for they were so severe.
   It is not right to impress a son or to try to hold him down,
   For it causes him for to leave his home when he is far too young.

4. Here's adieu unto another one, I mean my mother dear.
   [She reared a son who fell as soon as he left her tender care.]
   It's little did she think when she sang sweet lullaby
   Which country I might travel in or what death I might die.

5. Here's adieu unto Prince Edward's Isle and that island girl so true.
   Long may she live to view the spot where first my breath I drew.
   No more I'll watch those gallant ships as they go sailing by
   With their banners high up in the air far above their canvas high.

6. There's one request I ask of you and that one I do pray.
   May the Heavenly Father bless the spot where my moldering bones do lay.
   But times will roll on just the same as before I passed away.
   What signifies the life of one whose moldering bones are clay?

This favorite ballad of the Maritime lumbermen describes the fate of young Peter Amberley (or Emberley), who died near Boiestown, New Brunswick, early in 1881. The verses were composed by John Calhoun, a local poet who had known Amberley. He sent them to a neighbor, Abraham Munn, to put a tune to them, and Munn is believed to have added the stanza about craving a holy father to bless the grave. Angered by this addition, Calhoun printed several hundred broadsides of his version, which helped to spread the ballad.

Although very well known all along the east coast, the song has rarely wandered inland. Beck reports that the shantyboys of Michigan,

Minnesota, and Wisconsin "are not unfamiliar with 'Peter Ambelay,' " but the only version he quotes comes from a Nova Scotia man.

Several Maritime texts run to ten stanzas, with Joe Thibadeau's eight stanzas representing the average. The six that Martin McManus remembered correspond to those sung by Marie Hare, which Edward Ives calls the "hard core" of the ballad. Leo Spencer also knew "Peter Emery," as it is always called in Ontario.

The Ontario tunes all belong to the family commonly used for "The *Flying Cloud*." Martin McManus's is a fairly elaborate form, resembling a rare song, "Rich Amerikay" (O 19), found in Newfoundland and the Catskills.

References

PRINTED. Laws, *NAB*, 160. Creighton, *SBNS*, 301–303. Gray, 63–69. Manny, 160–163. Wilson, 82–83.

RECORDED. Folk Legacy FSC 9 (Hare). Folkways FM 4053 (Wilmot MacDonald), FE 5323 (Ives), FW 6821 (Hemsworth). National Museum FO 4-40 (Spencer), FO 4-41 (McManus).

Tune Relatives

Barry, 32. Bayard, 15–16, 42. H. P. Beck, 247. Belden, 128, 138. Cazden, *Abelard* I, 44, 123 n. Colcord, 145. Creighton, *SBNS*, 187. Doerflinger, 136. Hugill, 586. Peacock, 816. Petrie, nos. 418, 419, 420. Ranson, 46. Rickaby, 145. Folk Legacy FSC 10 (I–7).

37. The River through the Pine (dC 33)

A

Sung by Bob McMahon
Peterborough, Ontario   October 1959

1. Oh, Mary was as fair a girl as the flowers that bloom in spring—
   She was fairer than the roses that bloom all in the early spring.
   Her heart was full of happiness on this mornin' fair and fine;
   Her lover was a driver on the river through the pine.
2. Now Charlie held a peavey with the driver's hand and skill;
   He swung an axe with vengeance in that northern country still.
   He labored all the summer, all the winter in the pine,
   And they called him Charlie Williams from the town of Brandywine.
3. But Charlie and his Mary they got married in the spring
   When the trees were buddin' early and the birds began to sing.
   Now Mary's heart grew happy and her eyes with love did shine
   For her young and handsome husband from the town of Brandywine.

4. "It's now I must leave you, dear, with the sense of awful love,
To go and make some money for my fond and turtle dove.
I'll drive the lonesome river all the summer fair and fine,
Return and see you, Mary, when the fruit is on the vine."

5. As early one morning in Wisconsin's early clime,
He ran the northern rapids on the river through the pine.
He had no time to tarry: soon the blow of awful death,
Those ragged rocks and waterfalls, deprived him of his breath.

6. They found his body floatin' on this mornin' fair and fine—
Charlie Williams he had perished on the river through the pine.
"I'll write a letter to her though I know she soon will pine,"
Said a friend of Charlie Williams on the river through the pine.

7. Now when she received this letter her eyes no more did shine
. . . .
. . . .
. . . .

8. Every raft of timber that goes down the Chippewa,
His grave it is visited by drivers on their way.
On his grave we planted wild flowers and trimmed the wayward vine,
On the grave of Charlie Williams on the river through the pine.

B "The Town of Brandywine"

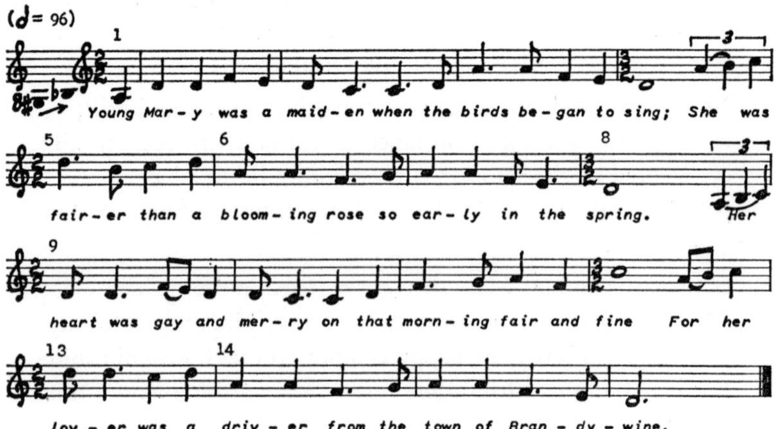

Sung by Dominic Foran
Quyon, Quebec November 1966

1. Young Mary was a maiden when the birds began to sing;
She was fairer than a blooming rose so early in the spring.
Her heart was gay and merry on that morning fair and fine
For her lover was a driver from the town of Brandywine.

2. Young Charlie used the peavey with the driver's hand and skill,
And he swung an axe with energy in the northern forest still.
He would labor all the winter and the summer in the pine,
And they called him Charlie Williams from the town of Brandywine.

3. Young Mary she got married to her lover in the spring
When the buds began to blossom and the birds began to sing.
"Now darling, I must leave you in the happiness of love.
I must make some V's and X's for you, my blooming dove.
I will labor all the winter and in summer in the pine;
I'll return to you, my darling, when the fruit is on the vine."

4. Young Mary she was faded and no more was gazed upon,
For the happiness of her maiden dreams his wild career had run,
And early one morning on Wisconsin's dreary clime
He had run those noisy rapids for his last sad fatal time.

5. They found his body lying on the rocky shores below
Where the noisy waters ripple and the silent cedars grow.
"I would send to her a letter, but I'm afraid she'd repine,"
Said a friend of Charlie Williams from the town of Brandywine.

6. Now every raft of timber that goes down the Chippewa
His lonesome grave is visited by drivers on their way.
They will plant wild flowers o'er his grave and pluck the weaving vines

O'er the grave of Charlie Williams from the town of Brandywine.

7. In a distant city I visited not many months ago—
It was in a southern climate where strange faces come and go—
I saw a gray-haired damsel, and no more her eyes did shine:
She's the widow of young Williams from the town of Brandywine.

8. She smiled as she saw me although she looked old and gray.
"I'm prepared to meet my river-boy," those words to me did say,
"And it's early in the autumn when the fruit is on the vine
I will welcome back my river-boy from the town of Brandywine."

(The last two lines of stanza 3 sung to the first half of the tune.)

This account of a raftsman's death on a Wisconsin river is very rare. The only text previously published was a manuscript copy sent to Rickaby. The versions here, recorded more than thirty years later, are at least as well preserved. Bob McMahon's lacks the two-verse postscript in which the singer meets Mary long after Williams' death, but it adds the graphic second stanza that names Brandywine as Williams' home and it fills out stanzas 3 and 4, which were run together into a single six-line stanza in the Rickaby text. Dominic Foran's text is unusual in omitting any reference to "the river through the pine" but is otherwise comparable with Rickaby's. His tune is also like Rickaby's, whereas Mr. McMahon's differs, being related to the "Peter Emery" tune used in Ontario.

In addition to Rickaby's version, Beck gives this fragment in *They Knew Paul Bunyan*:

It was down the logging stream
Down along the Chippeway,
There's a silent grave that's visited
By drivers on the way.

He takes this to be a stanza of "Turner's Camp," but it is obviously from the last stanza of "The River through the Pine." Sidney Robertson and Alan Lomax recorded the ballad from Frank Uchytil for the Library of Congress, and Ray C. Calkins of Phillips, Wisconsin, sang it at the National Folk Festival in Denver, May 6, 1966.

References

PRINTED. Laws, *NAB*, 261 (Rickaby, 119–121). E. C. Beck, *Bunyan*, 43. Lomax, *North America*, 113 (reprinted from Rickaby).

RECORDED. Library of Congress AFS 1662–3, AFS 3246, AFS 3253–4 (Uchytil). National Museum FO 19-182 (McMahon).

Tune Relatives

A. See Song 36.
B. Rickaby, 119. Wilson, 22 (no. 12).

38. The Grand River (dC 35)

Sung by Johnny Flanagan
Erinsville, Ontario October 1960

1. It was down on the Grand River near a place called Lake Chayere.
   Four young men got in a boat and forward they did steer.
   Their intention was to row the falls, their course they did pursue,
   Their boat ran with quick motion, and from it they went through.

2. A small boy standing on the beach that awful sight did view.
   Straightway to their dear parents the message quicklie flew.
   Fathers and mothers, brothers and sisters too,
   Came running down unto the bank to see if it was true.

3. Both day and night it sounded amongst those hellish springs,
   But nothing of their bodies in any shape were seen
   Until nine days were over their floating corpses were spied
   Amongst those hellish rocks where the watery waters flow [flowing waters glide].

"The Grand River" is another tragic ballad that has previously been printed only by Rickaby. He gives it as a five-stanza unnamed fragment sent to him by a North Dakota woman whose father had been a woodsman in Canada and Minnesota. Johnny Flanagan's first two stanzas correspond to the first and third in Rickaby's text; his third is different. The only other report is a Library of Congress recording made in Michigan in 1938.

What Mr. Flanagan gives as "a place called Lake Chayere" reads "near the falls of Chaudière" in Rickaby's text, indicating an Ontario origin (Chaudière Falls lie just below Lake Nipissing). The ballad is rare in Ontario, for Mr. Flanagan, then eighty, is the only one who has sung it for me. His tune is an old Irish one that has also turned up in New Brunswick and Newfoundland.

References

PRINTED. Laws, *NAB*, 261 (Rickaby, 129–130).

RECORDED. Library of Congress AFS 3399 (Alfred Osborne). National Museum FO 20-193 (Flanagan).

Tune Relatives

Galvin, 34. Joyce, *OIFM*, no. 53. Manny, 276. O'Neill, no. 169. Peacock, 105, 187, 592. Wilson, 34 (nos. 28, 28a).

39. The Haggertys and Young Mulvanny

Sung by Lennox Gavan
Quyon, Quebec November 1966 and August 1968

1. One pleasant evening as I did wander
   When the trees and blossoms were all in bloom,
   And the pleasant odor from off the treetops
   Did scent the air with its sweet perfume,
   All nature seemed to be early smiling,
   The forest's green leaves were spreading wide,
   And the branching shadows from sprouting treetops
   Did burst the meadows from every side.

2. The shades of evening did streak the landscape,
The silvery moon did appear in view,
And beyond the crest of yon green-topped mountains
Where the setting sun bid each scene adieu
My thoughts did wander to seek some pleasure
As e'er those fields grew more dim each day;
At yonder forest I gazed in silence
Where nature shines her last gleam of ray.

3. I spied a maiden in melancholy:
She wrang her hands, weeping in despair,
And the mournful cries of this youthful damsel
Reechoed loud through the balmy air,
For to greet the name of her own dear brother
In deep despair she did recall,
And the crystal teardrops as they descended
Did moist the earth on which they did fall.

4. My curiosity it was excited
To find the cause of her grief and woe,
And by enquiring from this fair damsel
Her sad reply soon gave me to know
That her tears did fall for the young Mulvanny,
Who lost his life on the Kipawa stream:
Both great and humble by all who knew him,
He never failed for to gain esteem.

5. Three brave young hearts on the stream did perish,
Her own dear brother being one of these,
And the other two being sons of a widow
Who I'll inform you were Haggertys.
Their reckless deeds caused their own destruction,
Being prompt and ready at every call,
They were the first of the crew selected
To guide that boat o'er the waterfall.

6. With hearts undaunted and courage equal
They did attempt this rash deed to do.

Unconscious were they and also careless
Of the event they were to ensue.
And as they steered her with noble courage,
Their fatal dangers not understood,
They were capsized by a raging billow
And soon engulfed in that mighty flood.

7. With anxious eyes watching every motion
Till in a mist they were lost to gaze,
A spray ascended from off the torrent
And rising up in a smokelike haze.
Their sympathizing friends stood all around them
The scenes of horror from shore to view,
Till the cruel billows closed o'er their bodies,
And from this world caused them bid adieu.

8. The whole raft's crew did that day assemble
To search the bottom from shore to shore
Beneath the foot of those noisy rapids
Where surging waters do steadily roar,
And as they searched in the still clear water,
Which was only ruffled by a summer's breeze,
The first result of their eager searching
Was finding two of the Haggertys.

9. And not long after they found Mulvanny:
Beneath the green leaves his body lay,
With little pebbles lying all around him,
And little fishes all around him played.
Prostrated low in the sandy bottom
Where nothing dwelt but the fiendish brood,
His curly locks were surging the waters
Moved all around by that restless flood.

10. Now far away up the distant river
Their graves were dug by the rolling tide
Beneath the branches of swaying treetops
Moved by the breezes from every side.

Yes, far away up that distant river
No sound could reach any mother's ear,
And raindrops fell on them from the branches
Instead of parents' lamenting tears.

11. Now melancholy each autumn season
Will be renewed by the changing woods,
And trees and flowers resume their pleasure
And drop their dry leaves like warriors' blood.
Brown and withered and drooping downward
Those virgin green leaves forever lost,
So were those young men cut down while blooming
Just like the flowers of an early frost.

This ballad of a river tragedy is much more elaborate than the many other lumbering ballads that tell a similar story. Its language is obviously inspired by romantic Irish ballads like "Youghal Harbour," whose tune it borrows.

I first came across this song when Bernie Bedore printed a four-stanza text from Mrs. Walter Smith of Calabogie in the *Renfrew Advance* (November 14, 1963). He noted: "Mick McHale of Douglas, long a shanty foreman for McLaughlin, sang for me a verse of the song, and Alec Culhane of Killaloe, another McLaughlin man, told me the story of how Jimmy the Duck pulled his boat into an eddy to bail but Haggarty and Mulvannon failed to stop to do so and went to their deaths." Three years later Lennox Gavan of Quyon, Quebec, sang the first six stanzas for me and allowed me to copy the others from a notebook in which his sister had written the song as their mother sang it. Then in August 1968 Mr. Gavan sang the whole song at the Mariposa Folk Festival and taped it for me. Francis Bennett of Quyon also sang it, and except for some missing lines his version paralleled Mr. Gavan's, even to the poetic imagery of the last two stanzas.

The scene of the tragedy was the Kipawa River, which drains Lake Kipawa into the Ottawa River just north of Timiskaming. Mr. Gavan calls the song "The Kipawa Stream," but because that is the title of another song (63), I have kept the title Mrs. Smith used. Neil Mulvenna of Blind River wrote to the *Renfrew Advance* (November 21, 1963) that his father's brother, Matt Mulvenna, was one of the men drowned and that the accident happened before 1902, although he did not know the exact date.

Tune Relatives

Creighton, *SBNS*, 99. Creighton and Senior, 110. Edwards, 30. Galvin, 28. Ives, *Larry Gorman*, 32. Joyce, *OIFM*, nos. 422, 680. Leach, 90. Manny, 102, 294. O'Lochlainn, 16, 156. O'Neill, no. 206. Petrie, nos. 75, 252, 1069. Sandburg, 360–361. Wilson, 23 (nos. 15, 15a). Riverside RLP 12-602 (II–2). Topic 12T139 (II–5).

40. Bill Dunbar

Sung by Joe Thibadeau
Bobcaygeon, Ontario October 1964

1. Come all you sympathizers, I pray you lend an ear.
   It's of a drownding accident as you shall quicklie hear.
   It's the drowning of Bill Dunbar, a man you all know well—
   He lived in the village of Kinmount where he ran a big hotel.

2. Bill Dunbar was a noble man as you may understand—
   Kind-hearted and obliging, a powerful able man.
   It made no difference what you profess, he would always treat you well.
   There was no danger of being insulted in Dunbar's big hotel.

3. They drove down to attend the races, as you may understand,
   Returning home all from the same, he and Bob Cunningham.
   The night being dark, they lost their way, which grieves me to relate:
   They drove into Gannon's Narrows at the foot of Pigeon Lake.

4. The team was lost, both men were drowned, which is hard for to unfold,
It being in the depths of winter and the water piercing cold.
Poor Bill he fought hard for his life, as I have heard them say;
He threw his mitts out on the ice as a token where he lay.

5. It was on a Tuesday evening they met with their sad doom,
And their bodies were not recovered until Thursday afternoon.
They were taken home to Kinmount; large crowds did gather there—
The people came from far and near when they heard of the sad affair.

6. Bill Dunbar in his former days was foreman for Mossom Boyd
And many the river he did run, both narrow, deep, and wide.
He was never known to send a man where danger would draw near,
But he boldlie took the lead himself without either dread or fear.

7. Bill leaves a wife and one small child in sorrow, grief, and pain;
Likewise his brothers and sisters in sorrow to remain.
In meditation they are left, which grieves them to the heart,
That it should ever come their lot that he would from them part.

8. He's gone the road we all must go, let the time come short or long,
So I'll drop my pen, likewise conclude my sentimental song,
Hoping to meet on a better shore where trials they are few,
Where we shall return in happiness old acquaintance to renew.

This local Ontario ballad has enjoyed considerable popularity throughout the Peterborough region. It describes a tragedy that happened in 1894: Bill Dunbar and Bob Cottingham of Kinmount were drowned when their sleigh broke through the ice of Gannon's Narrows in Pigeon Lake as they were returning from attending ice races at Peterborough. The two men are buried in the Kinmount cemetery. Dunbar's grandson, Leon Wright, still lives in Kinmount and has in his possession the mitts mentioned in the song. Mossom Boyd, for whom Dunbar worked, was the first man to settle in the Sturgeon Lake region; he was a very successful lumberman who died in 1883.

Both Joe Thibadeau and Emerson Woodcock say that the song was composed by Dave Curtin, a lumberman and "walking boss" well known in the 1890's. Most of the former shantyboys in and around Peterborough knew or had heard the ballad: in addition to Thibadeau and Woodcock, I have it from Martin Sullivan of Nassau and Mrs. Tom Sullivan of Lakefield. All have the same eight stanzas, showing only minor verbal differences, and all change Bob Cottingham's name to "Cunningham." The tunes vary somewhat: Mr. Thibadeau's is related to "Brennan on the Moor" and Mr. Woodcock's to "The Wild Colonial Boy."

REFERENCES

RECORDED. Folkways FM 4052 (Woodcock). National Museum FO 8-72 (Martin Sullivan); FO 8-73 (Mrs. Tom Sullivan).

TUNE RELATIVES

Barry, 62. H. P. Beck, 254. Cazden, *Abelard* I, 72, 109 n. Creighton, *SBNS*, 179. Creighton and Senior, 236. Edwards, 36, 72. Fowke, 94 (and Folkways FM 4005, II–12). Galvin, 48. Joyce, *OIFM*, no. 379. Manny, 254. O'Lochlainn, 126. Peacock, 66. Randolph I, 81–82. Sharp I, 377; II, 170. Thomas, 152.

41. The Cold Black River Stream

A
Sung by Leo Spencer
Lakefield, Ontario August 1957

1. Come you shantymen and drivers, come listen one and all.
Your sympathy I do invoke, your attention I will call
To the sad fate of a young man who from Peterborough came,
Who lost his life on McCormick's drive on the Black River stream.

2. On the eleventh day of April to his home he bid farewell
In company with his brother, and the truth to you I'll tell.
His fond and loving mother begged of him home to remain,
And warned him of the danger on the Black River stream.

3. But alas, alas, it was in vain. Oh, at home he would not stay,
But to that ill-fated river his course he steered away.
He was young, he was in his bloom, and of danger did not dream
That fatal day would meet his death on the cold Black River stream.

4. But a nobler crew, the truth I'll tell, this route had never run.
'Twas the Peterborough and Lindsay boys for merriment and fun,
But now their hearts are sad and sore since death amongst them came
And leaves their crew a number less on the Black River stream.

5. He left his camp that morning his labor to pursue.
'Twas the fate that did await him, and alas he little knew.
In jumping from a log he fell, the truth I will explain:
As he could not swim, to the bottom sank on the cold Black River stream.

6. What an awful sight it was for those who witnessed it from the shore!
This young and manly hero died, and his fate they did deplore.
Three times he rose invoking help, but alas, it was in vain,
As he could not swim, to the bottom sank of the cold Black River stream.

7. What an awful sight their gaze did meet when his body it was found!
His comrades gently bore him out and placed him on the ground.
The lifeless form so still and cold one deathly smile did beam,
Till the silent lips was ever closed by the Black River stream.

8. What his brother's feelings they would be as he gazed in mute despair
On the cold form of him he loved, and his moans would pierce the air.
On him in life he loved so dear his bitter tears did stream

As he knelt beside him on the banks of the cold Black River stream.

9. He had the form of her he loved bending there his face to see.
To embrace one kiss on his cold lips what would her anger [anguish] be?
She gently smoothed his damp cold locks while to his breast did strain,
His lifeless form she did embrace at the cold Black River stream.

10. No more his laugh or his songs is heard like ones we used to hear
On the merry stream come rafted down the river to our ears.
He's gone, and peace be to his soul, for his spirit knows no pain.
He met his death on the treacherous steps of the cold Black River stream.

11. This young man's name was Corkery, and the truth I will pen down,
As he was well known and well beloved all around Peterborough town.
He left his home in the bloom of youth; far better he had remained
Than to meet his death on those treach waters called *the Black River stream*.

B

Sung by George McCallum
Grafton, Ontario March 1961

1. You boys and drivers come sympathize with me,
And kindly pay attention to those old words I say.
It's all about a young man from Peterborough came.
He was drownded on McCormick's drive on the cold Black River stream.

2. He was jumping from a log one day, accidentally he went in,
. . . .
. . . .
And 'twas heaven's decree his death would be on the cold Black River stream.

3. They pulled him from his watery grave, combed down his curly hair,
 And the girl that loved him dearly, she cried all in despair.
 She said, "My dearest Jimmy, how strange it all does seem,
 But it was heaven's decree your death would be on the cold Black River stream."

4. 'Twas early the next morning his body was sent home.
 When his poor old mother she saw him, she dropped down like a stone.
 She said, "My dearest Jimmy, how strange it all does seem,
 But it was heaven's decree your death would be on the cold Black River stream."

This further example of the Ontario elegiac ballad had some hold in tradition, for two different versions have survived. Both agree on the main facts: a young man from Peterborough was drowned on a drive on the Black River while working for McCormick—probably Andrew McCormack, a well-known Ottawa lumberman who in the 1860's brought many drives down the rivers flowing into the Ottawa. The details are less clear: one version gives the boy's first name as Jimmy, the other his last name as Corkery (possibly Corcoray); the accident happened on the eleventh of April, but no year is mentioned.

Leo Spencer uses a one-line tune, repeating it four times with but slight variation (Barry has almost the same tune for "The Burning of Henry K. Robinson's Camp"), whereas George McCallum uses a similar two-line tune repeated twice.

REFERENCES

RECORDED. National Museum FO 20-191 (Spencer), FO 20-192 (McCallum).

TUNE RELATIVES

Barry, 48. Manny, 181.

42. Young Conway

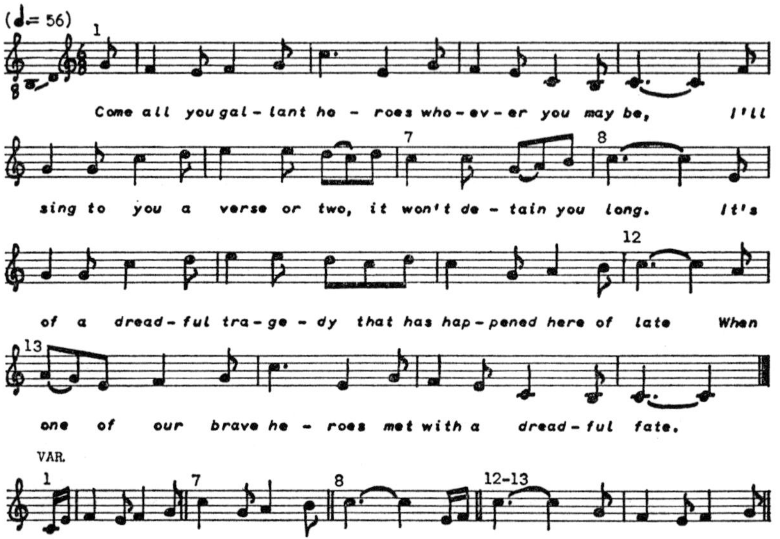

Sung by Michael Cuddihey
Hull, Quebec March 1965

1. Come all you gallant heroes whoever you may be,
   I'll sing to you a verse or two, it won't detain you long.
   It's of a dreadful tragedy that has happened here of late
   When one of our brave heroes met with a dreadful fate.

2. On the thirteenth of September last he left his native home;
   In company with his brother-in-law to the shanty he was goin'.
   He changed his mind in Pembroke, and then he turned around,
   And he set out for Renfrew, it being his favorite town.

3. That night whilst in Renfrew he went to a Poland spree
   In company with his brother-in-law and likewise Tom McGee.
   Our hero being light-hearted, for pleasure he was bent.
   To spend a quiet and peaceful night it was his whole intent.

4. Young Mulby and a Poland, they raised a little fuss.

They jostled around quite manfully till Ned gave him the worse.
Another Poland interfered; Ned Mulvay then struck him,
And scarcely was the blow given till the slaughter did begin.

5. Now our hero he being sitting down, he cried out for peace.
He sprang upon those cowardly dogs his comrades to release.
Those cowardly dogs being angry and blood being their delight,
They all turned on poor Conway, his comrades put to fright.

6. But ten to one was hardly fair. They brought him to his knees,
But he being young and manfully his way did upward squeeze.
The second time they brought him down they stabbed him o'er and o'er,
And a stroke of a tomahawk on the head they laid him on the floor.

7. From three o'clock that morning till four o'clock next day
Our hero he did thus remain, it being a mournful day.
At four o'clock he departed, took a tear from every eye,
And his poor old mother being there, it was hard to hear her cry.

8. He had the largest funeral that e'er to Douglas came—
Four and twenty young men, and they all dressed the same.
They conveyed him to St. Mary's church and laid his body low,
And a tear did fall from every eye that did poor Conway know.

9. Now for his brave and manly deeds his enemies they were few,
And except for those cowardly dogs I hope they'll be put through.
I hope that God will pardon him and grant him this request:
When he reaches the eternal shore, in heaven his soul *may rest.*

Still another elegiac ballad, "Young Conway" varies the pattern by describing a young shantyboy who was killed in a brawl rather than on the river. It seems to have been more widely known than either "Bill Dunbar" or "The Cold Black River Stream." I have three versions from different regions: Michael Cuddihey's home north of Ottawa, Emerson Woodcock's in Peterborough (nearly two hundred miles away), and a third copy in the notebook of Gertie Mercier of Foresters Falls, between Arnprior and Pembroke. All follow the same pattern with many small differences, the most notable being the variation in date, which is given as September 13, November 14, and December 18—none of which is right. All give Renfrew as the scene of the fight: indeed, Miss Mercier calls the ballad "The Renfrew Murder," and all have the hero buried in St. Mary's church, though only Mr. Cuddihey indicates that it is in Douglas, a town a dozen miles west of Renfrew.

Mr. Cuddihey said that he didn't know whether he should sing this song. When asked why, he said it used to cause fights in the camps between the Irish and Polish shantyboys. He learned it in about 1910 when working for Guinness on the Coulonge River.

Thanks to Father Joseph E. Gravelle, the details of the tragedy have been uncovered. The following account is condensed from his letter in the *Renfrew Advance*, November 18, 1965.

On January 17, 1886, a wedding took place in Renfrew and the festivities which followed this event were held at the home of Matthew Dzonkoski . . . Without receiving an invitation entitling him to attend, a young Douglas man, Michael Conway, . . . along with two companions, decided to join the party. . . . These three young men were well intentioned and certainly meant no harm. They brought a gift for the bride, which they left covered outside until the most suitable time to make the presentation. When this moment arrived and the gift, a baby carriage, was carried in, turmoil broke out. They found that all nations do not have the same sense of humor. In the brawl knives were drawn and the unwelcome visitors tried to make their escape. One darted through an open window, the other two got through the back door, but only one succeeded in getting over the fence. The other, young Conway, was stabbed to death and his body thrown over the fence. . . . No criminal action was taken, for the reason that it would be impossible to determine which of the twenty wounds really caused his death, and who was the man who struck the fatal blow.

The tune used for "Young Conway," like that of "Save Your Money While You're Young," is a version (in major) of the Catskill "I Walked the Road Again," which O'Neill gives for "The Bonny Laboring Boy" and Joyce has for "My Irish Molly O."

References

RECORDED. National Museum FO 8-76 (Woodcock).

TUNE RELATIVES

Barry, 33. Cazden, *Abelard* I, 4–5; *NYFQ* 16 (1960), 100. Creighton, *MFS*, 147, 185; *SBNS*, 165. Edwards, 28. Fowke, 120, 134 (and Folkways FM 4052, II–9). Hughes III, 16–18. Ives, *Larry Gorman*, 103–104. Joyce, *OIFM*, no. 403. Leach, 122. Manny, 99. O'Neill, nos. 195, 577. Ranson, 102. Folkways FM 4053 (II–2). Riverside RLP 12-602 (I–5).

43. Vince Leahy

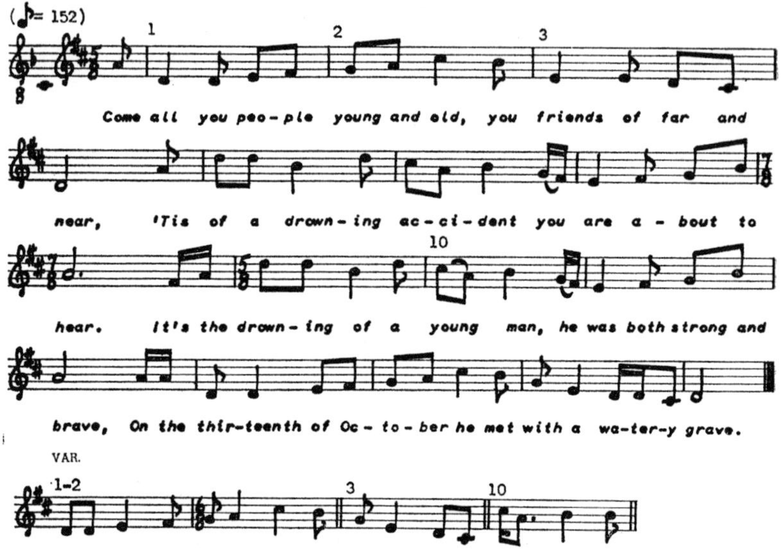

Sung by Dave McMahon
Peterborough, Ontario March 1957

1. Come all you people young and old, you friends of far and near,
 'Tis of a drowning accident you are about to hear.
 It's the drowning of a young man, he was both strong and brave,
 On the thirteenth of October he met with a watery grave.

2. For six long months that summer, if I remember right,
 He worked on the construction of the logs at Youngs's Point.
 'Twas when those logs were finished and his horses he brought home,
 Then taking off their harness, he turned them free to roam.
 He then went as a laborer on the dam of Number Four
 And lost his life in the raging boils down by that Smithtown shore.

3. When he left home that morning, his heart was light and gay,
 And his kind and loving mother begged him home with her to stay.

He only joked and laughed with her, which pleased her for awhile.
'Twas little she was thinking that's the last she'd see him smile.

4. He worked away from early morn till late that afternoon,
And just before the sun went down he met his fatal doom.
He slipped into a stop-log place, as I have just been told—
'Twas in the days of autumn, and the water piercing cold.

5. This young man fought hard for his life, as I have heard them say.
He caught the rope they threw to him but was quickly swept away.
His comrades tried to rescue him, but efforts were in vain,
For he sank beneath those cruel waves and never rose again.

6. Through all that long and lonesome night in the riverbed he lay,
And searchers found his body about eight o'clock next day.
They took him from his watery grave unto the shore near by,
And his poor old agéd mother, it was hard to hear her cry.

7. This young man's name was Leahy, the truth I will pen down.
He was well known and dearly loved near Peterborough town.
'Twas for his brave and manful deeds he had gained a host of friends,
And with his widowed mother he lived by the river's bend.
He played beside its pleasant banks from he was but a child;
He never thought he'd meet his death in its waters cruel and wild.

8. He leaves his seven brothers in sorrow, grief, and pain;
Two sisters and his mother in sorrow to remain.
But he's gone a road we all must go; let the time be short or long.
I'll drop my pen, likewise conclude my sentimental song.
He's gone to a far better land where the partings they are few,
And I hope we'll meet Vince Leahy there, old acquaintance *to renew.*

(The last two lines of stanzas 2, 7, and 8 repeat the second half of the tune.)

This is a sample of an elegiac ballad that did not pass into tradition. Dave McMahon composed it when Vince Leahy, a young Peterborough man, was drowned while working on a dam in 1927. Apparently he did not sing it often, for none of the other singers in the area had heard it. It is an interesting example of how new elegiac ballads were created by fragmenting older ones: the first stanza echoes "Jimmy Whelan," stanza 3 echoes "Harry Dunn," and the first line of stanza 5 and the last stanza were borrowed from "Bill Dunbar." The tune, like the one commonly used for "Harry Dunn," derives from "The Wild Colonial Boy."

References

RECORDED. National Museum FO 19-183 (McMahon).

Tune Relatives. See Song 34A.

THE LIGHTER SIDE

44. When the Shantyboy Comes Down

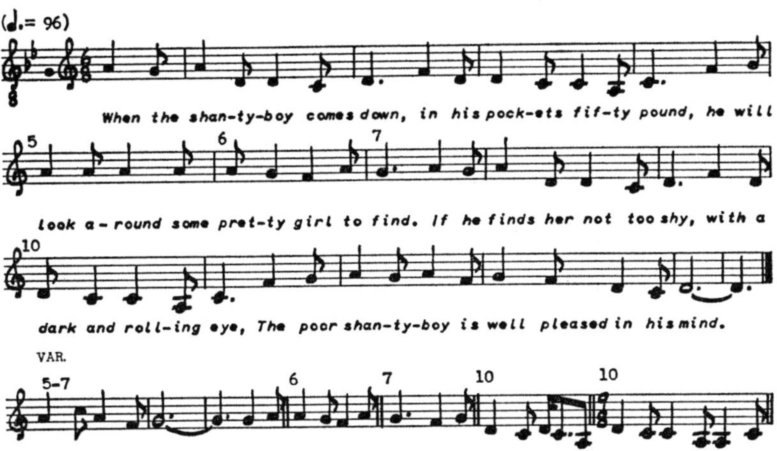

A

Sung by Jim Doherty
Peterborough, Ontario June 1957

1. When the shantyboy comes down, in his pockets fifty pound,
   He will look around some pretty girl to find.
   If he finds her not too shy, with a dark and rolling eye,
   The poor shantyboy is well pleased in his mind.

2. When the landlady comes in, she is neat and very trim;
   She is like an evening star.
   If she finds him in good trim, she is always ready to wait on him,
   And from one to two they'll sit up in the bar.

3. So the shantyboy goes on till his money is all gone
   And the landlady begins for to fret.
   So he says, "My lady, do not fret, I will pay my honest debt
   And bid adieu to the girl I had in town."

4. There's a gang in command, so the old folks understand,
   And it's for the back woods they are bound.
   With a whisky and a song we will shove our old canoe along,
   Bid adieu to the girl I had in town.

B

Sung by Leo Spencer
Lakefield, Ontario September 1962

1. When the shantyboy comes down, in his pocket fifty pound,
And he wanders for some little girl to find.
If he finds one not too shy, with a dark and rolling eye,
Then the shantyboy is well pleased in his mind.

2. The poor shantyboy goes on till his money it's all gone,
And the landlady began for to fret.
Says, "My darling, don't you fret, I will pay my honest debt,
Bid adieu to the girl I left in town."

This lumbercamp adaptation of the British sailors' ballad "Jack Tar on Shore" (K 39) is known on the east coast as "The Lumberman in Town." Fanny Eckstorm notes that it is "one of the finest of the old woods songs." It is also one of the rarest: apart from these Ontario versions, it had been reported from three men, all of whom learned it in the Maine woods. In addition to the version Mrs. Eckstorm noted in 1901, the Gordon manuscript has a text "as learned in the Maine woods in 1909" and Ives has published two versions from a Prince Edward Island singer who also learned it in Maine. All are quite similar to Jim Doherty's, except that they speak of a lumberman rather than a shantyboy and of crowns rather than pounds. They also add two melancholy stanzas carrying the lumberman through to old age. A west-coast version, "The Lumber-jack in Town," appears in the 1932 folio *Lumberjack Ballads*, compiled by Elmore Vincent, who was billed as "The Northwest Shanty Boy."

Mr. Doherty's tune is a derivative of "The Cruiskeen Lawn." Leo Spencer sings his abbreviated version to a variant of "Darling Nellie Gray."

References

PRINTED. Eckstorm, 96–97 (reprinted in Barry, 61; Gray, 58–59; Lomax and Lomax, *U.S.A.*, 172–173). Fowke and Johnston, 84–85 (same as above). Gordon MS, 263. Ives, *NEF* 2 (1959), 58–59; *NEF* 5 (1963), 68–70. Vincent, 4–5.

RECORDED. Folkways FM 4052 (Doherty).

TUNE RELATIVES

Cazden, *Abelard*, II, 72. Fowke, 16–17 (and Folkways FM 4051, I–12). Joyce, *OIFM*, no. 389. O'Neill, no. 254. Wilson, 39 (no. 32), 46 n.

45. How We Got Up to the Woods Last Year

A

Sung by Michael Cuddihey
Hull, Quebec March 1965

1. Come all you lads that would like to hear
   How we got up to the woods last year,
   Unto that place you all do know—
   That sunken hole called Opeongo.

REFRAIN

To me rantin' O, fal the diddle ay,
Rant and roar and drunk all the way.

2. On the thirteenth of September last—
   God be with those days that passed!—
   From Arnprior we did push out
   All with John Pratt to show us the route.

3. We travelled on till we came to Renfrew.
   'Twas there we met with the rest of the crew.
   Handsome boys both young and stout,
   The pick of the town there is no doubt.

4. To form an acquaintance we did begin.
   Some of the boys dip deep in the gin.
   Seven jolly boys got on a spree,
   And to hire a rig we did agree.

5. Some of us couldn't pay, some of us could,
   But anyway our name were good.
   Into that buggy we jerked our boots,
   And we made the teamster feed long oats.

6. You may depend we felt quite big
   In our silver-mounted rig.
   For Dacre town we hoist our sails,
   And they all thought there it was the Prince of Wales.

7. Mills came out to welcome us in:
   He handed down his wine and gin.
   The landlord's treat went merrily round,
   And we drank a health to Dacre town.

8. Dinner being ready, we all took place.
   The foreman he of course said grace,
   But Johnny Morin thought long to wait,
   And Laderoute Joe shoved up his plate.

9. "Be damned," said Morin, "It's good to be first.
   The man last served fares oft the worst."
   But Pratt himself the truth did own:
   The man fared best that got the bone.

B "How We Got Back to the Woods Last Year"
Sung by Emerson Woodcock
Peterborough, Ontario July 1957

1. Oh, come all you lads that would like to hear
   How we got back to the woods last year.
   'Twas a great big place you all might know,
   A great big lake called Michigan-I-O.

REFRAIN

To ma rant tam mana, fal the dooey-ay,
Rant ama roar and drunk on the way.

2. Now to hire a rig as we did begin,
Some of us took a drink of gin.
Well, the most of us got on a spree,
And to hire a rig as we did agree.

3. Well, we hired a silver-mounted rig—
Oh, my God, didn't we feel big!
We hoist our sails for Dacresville
And they thought there it was the Prince of Wales.

4. Well, we jogged along till we came down through—
'Twas there we met with the rest of our crew.
They were handsome lads both tall and stout,
And the pick of the town there was no doubt.

5. Old Bill came out for to welcome us in:
He handed out his wine and his gin.
Well, the landlord's toast went merrily around,
And we drank the health of Dacre town.

6. So when supper was ready we all took our place:
Of course our foreman he said grace.
When Lazerus Joe swore the truth to be known,
The man that's last gets all the bone.

Michigan singers recall this trip through northern Ontario as "Drunk on the Way." The shantyboys traveled from Arnprior, some thirty miles west of Ottawa, through Renfrew and Dacre, to Lake Opeongo in Algonquin Park—a distance of about one hundred miles. The trip probably took place in the 1870's or 1880's, before a railway was built through this lumbering region.

For a song lacking any dramatic incident, this has had quite a run in tradition. Michael Cuddihey's form, probably close to the original, is the most complete I found. (A Michigan text has three more stanzas: one naming some of the men, and two at the end telling how they got to the camp, stayed all winter, and then went home and thought of "the time we got drunk on the way.") Another Ontario singer, George Hughey of Peterborough, sang it in much the same form as Mr. Cuddihey. When O. J. Abbott learned it, it had lost three more stanzas but still retained the reference to Arnprior. Emerson Woodcock's version shows further deterioration: Lake Opeongo has become "a lake called Michigan-I-O," and Arnprior and Renfrew have disappeared. The changes from Beck's text through Mr. Cuddihey's, Mr. Abbott's, and Mr. Woodcock's provide a good illustration of how oral transmission affects a local ballad. All use the same tune, a variant of that for "My Grandmother's Advice."

Further evidence of this song's popularity is the fact that it inspired two quite different lumbering songs: "The Teams at Wanapitei" and "Conroy's Camp" (Songs 21 and 46).

REFERENCES

PRINTED. E. C. Beck, *Lore*, 316–318. Fowke and Johnston, 82–83.

RECORDED. Folkways FM 4052 (Abbott). National Museum FO 3-23 (Hughey), FO 3-24 (Woodcock).

TUNE RELATIVES

E. C. Beck, *Lore*, 316. Brown IV, 250–252. Creighton, *MFS*, 36; *SBNS*, 185. Fowke, 34 (and Folkways FM 4051, II–1). Randolph I, 383.

46. Conroy's Camp

(To the tune of Song 45.)

Sung by Lennox Gavan
Quyon, Quebec November 1966 and August 1968

1. We left the camp at half-past eight.
When we got to Waltham it was late,
And Fleury said, "Come on in, boys,
We'll drink some beer and make some noise."

REFRAIN
To me rant and ay, only forty miles a day.

2. Now Leo Vin on horseback came
Until Shiner he got lame,
And seeing that they had his trunk
He jumped right on to watch his junk.

3. Now Frankie Lumphrey, the long brute,
He passed us up at the Kilbute.
He passed us in the rumble seat—
All we could see was his front teeth.

4. Now Freddie Birchall he's too small,
He couldn't come with us at all.
To see Agnes he was inclined—
It broke his heart to stay behind.

5. Now Jack Couvret, the Nickaba king,
He asked for his time, the dizzy thing.
Conroy said, "You can go today,"
And then he said he'd sooner stay.

6. He come along with his white dog:
All you could hear was that big log.
He said that it was sixty-two,
But you know, my boys, that wasn't true!

7. Now Joe Lupine he'll soon be down
With his big black and Couvret's brown.

He should be here now pretty soon
For he left the camp last Friday noon.

8. Now Gavan and Perrier made the route,
And they changed their horses turn about.
Coming to Waltham they did cheer
While all the rest were drinking beer.

"Conroy's Camp" is a lively local variation on "How We Got Up to the Woods Last Year"; it might have been titled "How We Got Back from the Woods." Lennox Gavan said that his brother, Clifford Gavan of Chapeau, Quebec, composed it in the spring of 1931, when the men were coming home after spending the winter working in Tom Conroy's camp, forty miles up the Black River north of Waltham, which is just above Allumette Island on the north shore of the Ottawa River.

This is a good example of the kidding, or "codding" as they called it, that went on in the camps. Mr. Gavan knew the men mentioned—Frankie Lumphrey, who had protruding teeth, and Jack Couvret, who was always boasting about a big log he brought down.

Mr. Gavan sang four stanzas the first time I met him and added four more in August 1968.

47. The Little Brown Bulls (C 16)

Sung by Tom Brandon
Peterborough, Ontario October 1962

1. Down the long trail came McCluskey in view
   With the big spotted steers, they're the pets of the crew.
   They're long, lean, and lanky, girding six foot and nine—
   "Just the boys," cried McCluskey, "to handle our pine."
2. Along came Bull Garden when the skidding was full,
   And he out-logged the bush with his little brown bulls.
   They're short, fat, and stubby, girding six foot and three—
   "Just the boys," cried Bull Garden. "You're the buckos for me."
3. "The skidding is good and our timber is tall;
   Six logs to the thousand the contract does call,
   So come on, you two buckos, and make a day full,
   We'll skid three to one to the little brown bulls."
4. "Oh, no," said Bull Garden, "that you never can do,
   Though your big spotted steers are the pets of the crew.

I have twenty-five dollars, and that I will pull
When you skid one more log than my little brown bulls."

5. So the day was appointed, it quickly drew nigh,
Both eager, both willing their fortunes to try.
The day was appointed, it quickly drew round,
Found the judges and scalers out there on the ground.

6. "Turn in, boys, turn in, boys," the foreman did say,
"Come on, lads, come on, and we'll call it a day.
We've counted, we've measured, each man to his team,
And soon we will know who has kicked the high beam."

7. After supper was over, McCluskey appeared
With a belt he had made for his big spotted steers.
To make it he ripped up his best mackinaw—
He was forced to do so according to law.

8. "Hold on there, McCluskey, hold on for awhile,
For the big spotted steers they are beat by a mile.
You've skidded one hundred and not a log more;
Bull Garden has beat you by a couple of score."

9. The men how they cheered, and McCluskey he swore!
He tore yellow locks from his long waving hair,
Put his hand to his pocket, and a bill he did pull,
Saying, "Here is the bet to those little brown bulls."

10. Here's adieu to Bull Garden, to Sudbury John!
That's the best piece of skidding I ever saw done.
So fill up your glasses, lads, fill them right full,
And drink best of health to the little brown bulls!

One of the most popular songs in the northern lumberwoods, "The Little Brown Bulls" dates from the days when ox teams were used to haul the logs to the rivers. The contest described has not been pinned down: one singer told Rickaby that it took place "in Mart Douglas's camp in northwest Wisconsin in 1872 or 1873," but another told Beck that "it perpetuates a skidding match at Thayer Lumber Company near Fife Lake, Michigan."

The ballad was very well known in both Wisconsin and Michigan but it is rare farther east: the versions Eckstorm found in Maine all came by way of Wisconsin. Most versions are quite similar, though the older ones are usually several stanzas longer than the Ontario texts. The rivals are consistently McCluskey and Gordon or close variants, and the bet is always for twenty-five dollars, a month's pay in the 1870's. Usually the contract calls for "three logs to the thousand." Since it takes three sixteen-foot logs twenty inches in diameter at the top to produce a thousand feet of lumber, even the six logs mentioned here would be quite hefty. The mackinaw torn up to make the winner's belt is the heavy woolen jacket of brilliant plaid that was the standard garb of northern woodsmen.

The Ontario tune is another in the "Villikens" family. Elsewhere the ballad is sung to the tunes of "Down, Derry Down" or "The Rock Island Line."

REFERENCES

PRINTED. Laws, *NAB*, 154. Gard, 68–70. Vincent, 12–13.

RECORDED. Folkways FA 2019 (Eskin), FM 4001 (Robert Walker). Library of Congress AAFS L1 (Emery DeNoyer), AAFS L55 (Charles Bowlen), AAFS L56 (Carl Lathrop); see also *Checklist*, 228. National Museum, FO 3-21 (Brandon, from a different recording).

TUNE RELATIVES. See Song 23.

48. Holmes Camp

(To the tune of "Villikens and His Dinah".)

Sung by Earl Clarke
British Columbia 1963

1. It was early last April when the logging was done
I went to Fort Francis to join in the fun.
My intentions were good—one drink and no more—
But I ended up with a dozen or more.

2. Fort Francis Hotel I did make it my home.
After dropping my packsack I decided to roam,
To meet with the 'jacks and gather all news,
And also to buy me a bottle of booze.

3. Now I met with McPherson, McLeod, and McMann,
Skerton, Sam Brennen, Ken Ferguson,
Charlie Delaney, Sput Utters, Pat Ryan,
Ollie Olson, and the boys were all feeling fine.

4. Now whiskey and beer were the drinks of the day.
We'd logged off our limit in the most unique way,
And the drive to the Border we also took down—
You'd think we were anywhere else but in town.

5. After drinking awhile I was getting quite tight.
I decided to go and lay down for the night,
When I meets a young maiden so fair and so fine.
I said to myself, "Here's where I make some time."

6. I asked this young maid if to my room she would go.
Her answer was, "Yes, but I've a friend, don't you know?"
Then along comes McPherson so jolly and gay
To take my girl friend out of my way.

7. Now that we're back at the bush camps again,
I fear that something's gone wrong with my brain,
For my head it is spinning, my head it is sore—
I swear I'll never get drunk any more.

8. But the life of the logger is ofttimes quite dull—
He must have his drink and he must have his fun.
But there's no use complaining, there's no one to blame:
When we make our next stake we'll blow it again.

Mr. R. T. Wright of Vancouver learned this song from Earl Clarke, a transient cook he met in a western logging camp in 1963. Mr. Clarke, who had spent many years in logging camps and on ships in the Arctic, said it was sung in the Holmes logging camp north of Rainy River in western Ontario. Fort Frances is the largest town in the district. The Border is a mill on Rainy Lake near the international border between Ontario and Minnesota. The logs were driven from Grassy Lake to Bending Lake and White Otter Lake and then down the Turtle River through Mine Center Lake, reaching Rainy Lake after a drive of some three hundred miles.

The song develops one of the favorite shantyboy themes: the sprees they had when they hit a town after the long months in the woods. It is sung to the familiar tune of "Villikens and His Dinah."

Reference

PRINTED. Wright, *Spin* 3:9 (1965), 13.

49. The Backwoodsman (C 19)

Sung by Calvin Kent
Haliburton, Ontario May 1965

1. It's as well as I remember, 'twas the year of 'forty-five.
   I thought myself so thankful for to find myself alive.
   I harnessed up my horses, and I joined the Super crew,
   And I went a-hauling cordwood as I often used to do.

2. I might have hauled one load, I might have hauled four.
   I went down to Omemee, and I couldn't haul no more.
   The barroom it was open, the liquor flying free,
   And I drank one glass, another filled for me.

3. Oh, I met an old acquaintance, I dare not tell his name.
   He was going to a ball at night; I thought I'd do the same.
   He was going to a ball at night, the music sweetly played,
   And the boys and girls all danced till the breaking of the day.

4. Oh, I put the saddle on my arm, I struck out to the barn.
   I saddled up the old gray nag, not thinking any harm.

I saddled up the old gray nag, I rode away quite still,
And I never halted till I got to Downeyville.

5. Oh, when I got to Downeyville the night was far advanced.
I got up on the floor, thought I'd have a little dance.
The fiddler he was rested, and his arms were stout and strong,
Played "The Bluebells of Ireland" for four hours long.

6. Oh, my father followed after me, I heard the people say.
He must have had a spyglass, or he'd never have found the way.
He peeked in every keyhole where he could see a light
Till his old gray locks was covered with the dew of the night.

7. Oh, come all you old married men, I think you've danced enough.
Let us spend a half an hour, and we'll get a cash account.
We'll go home to our plows and whistle and we'll sing,
And you'll never catch us out on a spree like this again.

8. Oh, come all you old women who tell your tales about,
I pray you tell no tales on me, I'm bad enough without.
I pray you tell no tales on me—I'm sure it's not the first.
If the truth was only known, I'm sure I'm not the worst.

This tale of a lively country spree seems to have been sung first in Vermont early in the nineteenth century. From there it spread through all the northeastern states, as far south as North Carolina, and as far west as North Dakota and Saskatchewan. Though it is always localized and minor details vary, the many versions hew to a remarkably consistent pattern, and all are sung to much the same tune. This striking tune is probably responsible for the popularity of the rather uneventful ballad, and Calvin Kent's rendition is an excellent form of it.

The song was well known in Ontario. A version Emerson Woodcock knew, close to Mr. Kent's, also mentions Omemee and Downeyville, small towns in the Peterborough region. Seventy miles farther east Mr. Tom Powell of Napanee sang:

Early one morning at half past three
I wakened very early in the town of Napanee.

References

PRINTED. Laws, *NAB*, 156. Brown III, 397–399. Cox, 404. Grover, 176–177. Thompson, 263–264. Vincent, 42–43.

RECORDED. Folkways FA 2317 (James B. Cornett), FS 3809 (Vern Smelser), FM 4052 (Woodcock), FE 4312 (Robert Paul). National Museum FO 19-180 (Powell).

Tune Relatives

Bayard, 35. Cazden, *Abelard* I, 14, 110 n. Creighton, *MFS*, 112; *SBNS*, 284. Grainger, no. 192. Joyce, *OIFM*, nos. 208, 333. Leach, 208. Peacock, 679. Petrie, no. 808. Folkways FM 4052 (II–5).

50. Shannelly's Mill (dC 54)

(To the tune of Song 20.)

Sung by P. Taillon
Cornwall, Ontario August 1961

1. To you my kind friends and to you I'll relate,
   I'll tell you what happened to me in York state.
   When I got to Genore I got into a fight,
   And to skip a policeman I forced out the light.
   My pockets are empty, and the truth I will tell,
   And I'll sing you a song about Shannelly's Mill.

REFRAIN
Derry down, down, down derry day.

2. Oh, I met with McGuire, and for a job I inquired.
   He gave me a wink and a nod.
   Both eyes were black, and he knew I was a pill,
   And he told me right welcome round Shannelly's Mill.
3. Oh, springtime is come on, our logs are all in,
   Our sledges are broken, our horses are thin;
   For the boys they are merry, they cannot be ill
   For they always grudge it in Shannelly's Mill.
4. When winter is over it's home you will go.
   You'll think of your firm and young Charlis Munroe.
   You will think of your firm and young Charlis Munroe—
   Just work to Canadians wherever you go.

Dr. Robert A. Kaiser, the first to report this song, heard it in the fall of 1953 from Roy Arnold, then fifty-nine, who had learned it from his uncle. His version ran to ten stanzas, with more details on the wanderings of the somewhat rambunctious hero.

This Ontario version is apparently the second reporting of the song. It comes from eighty-year-old Mr. P. Taillon of Cornwall, who did not remember where he had heard it. The song seems related in spirit to such broadside ballads as "Erin Go Bragh" and "The Wild Irishman in London" and goes to the "Down Derry Down" tune given for "Hauling Logs on the Maniwaki." Textually it appears to be an offshoot of "John Whipple's Mill."

REFERENCES

PRINTED. Laws, *NAB*, 263 (Kaiser, *NYFQ* 11 [1955], 134). Cf. Laws C 20, "Blue Mountain Lake."

RECORDED. National Museum FO 19-184 (Taillon).

"John Whipple's Mill": Cazden, *Abelard* I, 102–103; Ives, *NEF* 7 (1965), 29–31; Shoemaker, 66–69.

51. I Went to the Woods

Sung by Stanley Botting
Naramata, British Columbia February 1958

1. Shure I went to the woods where I heard a big drum.
   "By the holy St. Patrick," says I, "that's a drum!"
   So I looked all around me, ne'er a drum could I see,
   But a red-headed bird eating down a big tree.

REFRAIN
Ral de fal de diddle dero, tee oddle I day.

2. Oh, the cold of this country no man can describe.
   Shure the cold piercing winds takes the bones from your hide.
   It flays you all over your hands and your face—
   Oh, God bless the poor Irishman who comes to this place!
3. The girls of this country I shurely don't bother,
   For they are as proud as old Lucifer's mother.

One twist of their lips and to them I can't come,
For I can't stand the sight of them all chewing gum.

4. Then there's a compound of raw cabbage they make,
Shure it would physic old Satan till his two sides would ache.
They ferment it and boil it and keep it for kraut,
And the stink it would reach you a mile from the house.

Like "A-Lumbering We Go," this is a song Stanley Botting learned from Charlie McLaughlin, an old Ontario shantyboy. McLaughlin said it was supposed to be the letter an Irishman, transplanted to Canada, was sending to his brother to tell him about this new country. Mr. Botting would sing only these four stanzas, indicating that there were others he wouldn't repeat. Both the tune and the pattern suggest that the song is related to "The Baskatong" (Song 16), also somewhat indelicate.

THE SHANTYBOY AND HIS GIRL

52. The Farmer's Son and the Shantyboy

Sung by Emerson Woodcock
Peterborough, Ontario July 1957

1. As I strolled out one evening just as the sun went down,
I walked along quite carelessly till I came to Gamebridge town.
I heard two lovers conversing as slowly I passed by:
The one she loved a farmer's son, and the other a shantyboy.

2. Now the one who loved a farmer's son these words I heard her say:
The reason why she loved him, at home with her he would stay.
He'd stay at home all winter, to the wildwoods he'd not go,
And when the spring it did come in, his land he'd plow and sow.

3. "Now for to plough and sow your land," the other girl did say,
"Your crop should prove a failure, and your debt you could not pay.
Your crop should prove a failure and, grain market it being low,
Ofttimes the bailiff will sell you out for to pay the debt you owe."

4. "As for the bailiff selling me out, you need not me alarm,
For there is no need of running in debt if you are on a good farm.
You'll grow your bread all of your own, don't work in storms and snow [rain],
While a shantyman has to work each day his family to maintain.

5. "Now a shantyman's life is a wearisome life: to the wildwoods he must go.
He is ordered out before daylight to face the frost and snow,
While happy and contented my farmer's son can lie
And tell to me some tales of love until the storm rolls by."

6. "Oh, I do hate those soft stalks," the other girl did say,
"For the most of them they are so green the cows might eat for hay.
Always so lazy they are known when they come into town
For all the small boys will run out, saying, 'Johnny, how are you down?' "

7. "Oh, I do love my shantyboy who goes up in the fall.
He is both stout and hearty and fit to stand a squall.
With pleasure I'll receive him in the spring when he comes down.
His money he'll share quite free with me when your farmer's son's got none."

8. "What I have said of your shantyboy, I did not mean it so,
For if ever I get a real good chance, with the shantyboy I will go.
And I'll leave behind your farmer's son, *his land to plow and sow.*"

(Tune of the last stanza: ABA.)

"The Farmer's Son and the Shantyboy" was one of the most popular songs in Ontario as well as throughout the lumbering regions of the northeastern United States. Most versions mention a local town in the first stanza but are otherwise very similar. In fact the eight stanzas are so standard that it seems likely they were spread on broadsides. The form is patterned on such British "debates" as "The Husbandman and the Servingman," later refashioned to tell of plowmen and gardeners or soldiers and sailors.

Other Ontario versions differ little from Emerson Woodcock's in text or tune, except that George Hughey's completes the faulty eighth stanza:

Oh, it's all I said about your shantyboy I hope you'll pardon me,
And from these ignorant habitants if ever I get free,
If ever I get free again, with a shantyboy I'll go:
I'll leave them broken-hearted, their lands to plow and sow,

and adds this final stanza, which also turns up in a Michigan text:

Here's a health to Dodge and Thompson; they're enterprising men,
And for their country's good I'm sure they're doing all they can.
Likewise to every shantyboy that makes the wildwoods ring,
That falls the pine in the winter time and drives it in the spring.

The tune, which is like the ones Belden, Rickaby, and Flanders give for this song, has been used also for "The Jam on Gerry's Rocks," "Peter Emberley," and other lumbering songs.

REFERENCES

PRINTED. Barry, 78–79. E. C. Beck, *Lore*, 163–166 (reprinted in E. C. Beck, *Bunyan*, 193–197). Belden, 443–445 (reprinted in Lomax, *North America*, 109–110). Campbell, *World-Lore* 1:6 (1926), 222–223 (collected in Ontario). Dean, 51–53 (reprinted in Lomax and Lomax, *American Ballads*, 446–447; Rickaby, 48–53). Eckstorm, 27–30. Flanders *et al.*, 166–169. Gardner, 264–265. Shoemaker, 215–217. Thompson, 258. Tolman, *JAF* 35 (1922), 400–401. From Ireland: Henry, no. 662.

RECORDED. Folkways FA 2354 (Stekert). Library of Congress AFS 2309 (Lester Wells), AFS 4202 (Warde H. Ford). National Museum FO 19-176 (O. J. Abbott), FO 19-177 (Hughey), FO 19-178 (Woodcock).

Tune Relatives

Barry, 22, 44, 68. Bayard, 49–52. H. P. Beck, 204, 255. Belden, 443. Cazden, *Abelard* I, 6, 115 n. Colcord, 203. Creighton, *MFS*, 200; *SBNS*, 301. Creighton and Senior, 198. Doerflinger, 229. Flanders *et al.*, 115, 166. Joyce, *OIFM*, no. 382. Kidson, 121. O'Lochlainn, 18. O'Neill, nos. 165, 262, 365, 394. Manny, 160, 166. Peacock, 181, 641. Petrie, nos. 498, 657, 868. Wilson, 30–34 (nos. 27, 27a–27t), 45 n. (and Folkways FM 4053, I–2). Folk Legacy FSC 9 (II–4) and record booklet, 28.

53. Jack Haggerty (C 25)

Sung by Tom Brandon
Peterborough, Ontario October 1962

1. My name is Jack Haggerty, from Glensville I came.
   There's no one to control me so there's no one to blame.
   I'll tell you a story without no delay
   Of a pretty fair maiden who stole my heart away.

2. My name is Jack Haggerty, I'm a raftsman by trade.
   My name is engraved on the rocks and sandbars.
   I'm the boy who stands high where the white water foams,
   But the thoughts of dear Anna keeps crossing my mind.

3. She is won, and I took her from the Flat River side.
   I truly intended to make her my bride.
   She's the blacksmith's daughter from the Flat River side,
   And I truly intended to make her my bride.

4. I gave her fine silks and the nicest of lace,
   The costliest of muslin herself to embrace.

I gave her my wages herself for to keep;
I deprived her of nothing I had on this earth.

5. One day on Flat River a note I received
Saying dear Anna she had me deceived.
She had married another who had long been delayed,
And the next time I met her she'd ne'er be a maid.

6. Now it's on her old mother I place all the blame.
She always intended to blacken my name.
She'd have soon broke the vows that God would have tied,
Causing me for to wander till the day that I died.

7. So adieu to Flat River—for me there's no rest.
I'll shoulder my peavey and go to the west.
I'll go to Muskegon some comfort to find,
Leaving Flat River and dear Anna behind.

8. So come all you young raftsmen with hearts kind and true,
Don't trust any woman—you're beat if you do,
And if you find one with those dark chestnut curls,
Just think of Jack Haggerty and his Flat River girl.

In tracing the origin of this ballad, Geraldine Chickering has shown it to be about real people, though the story it tells is not true. In the late 1860's Dan McGinnis was a suitor of Anne Tucker, a blacksmith's daughter who lived in Greenville, a logging town on the Flat River that drains southern Michigan's great pine belt. Apparently he composed the song to get even with Anne's fiance, George Mercer, who had been made foreman of the camp in which both McGinnis and Jack Haggerty worked, and he used Haggerty's name to conceal his own identity.

The ballad is naturally most common in Michigan, where Beck says it is the best known of the shanty ballads except for "The Jam on Gerry's Rocks" and "The Lumberjack's Alphabet." It has also spread far afield: it was known in Maine as early as 1890, and two cowboy versions have turned up in Texas. It was popular in Ontario, where I have recorded it four times. Tom Brandon's text, which he learned from his brother Everett, is fairly close to the Michigan versions though not as long as some of them. John Leahy's version (on Folkways FM 4052) shows some interesting changes. Whereas other texts feature Anne, a blacksmith's daughter with dark chestnut curls, Mr. Leahy's Flat River girl is named Lucy, is the daughter of a lockmaster, and has dark auburn curls, changes suggesting that some Ontario shantyboy had adapted the song to fit a local situation. Similarly LaRena Clark transfers the action to Gravenhurst, an Ontario town in Muskoka. All sing it to a variant of "Villikens and His Dinah."

REFERENCES

PRINTED. Laws, *NAB*, 159. Dorson, *FFMA* 8: 1 (1966), 18–20. Eckstorm, 124–126. Holbrook, 137–138. Pike, *JAF* 48 (1935), 344. Shoemaker, 218–219. Vincent, 14–15.

RECORDED. Folk Legacy FSC 10 (Brandon). Folkways FM 4052 (Leahy). Library of Congress AAFS L56 (John Norman). National Museum FO 3-22 (Brandon, from a different recording), FO 19-179 (Clark).

TUNE RELATIVES

Barry, 74. E. C. Beck, *Lore*, 141. Cazden, *Abelard* II, 100, 116–117 n. Manny, 66, 156, 185. Rickaby, 10. Wilson, 25–27.

54. The Gatineau Girls

Sung by O. J. Abbott
Hull, Quebec April 1960

1. I am a jolly shantyboy, I love to sing and dance.
   I wonder what my girl would say if she would see my pants.
   Fourteen patches on the knees and sixteen on the stern,
   I wear them while I'm in the woods, and home I do return.

REFRAIN

I'm on my jovial way, and I spend my money free.
I have plenty, come and drink lager beer with me.

2. I like the girls of the Gatineau, they are so trim and neat.
   They are so slim around the waist; their kisses are so sweet.

There's Mary Ann and Josephine and likewise Jenny too—
Along with some of the Gatineau girls I'll roam this country through.

3. We often go on dancing—we dance all night, you see—
And often all the girls they grow very fond of me.
We dance all night till broad daylight, we dance until the morn—
Head and tail up like a steer running through the corn.

Though many other songs tell of "the jolly shantyboy," few are as light-hearted as this. Beck includes it as the first item in his *Lore of the Lumbercamps*, but his note indicates that it was recited rather than sung in Michigan. In his *Cowboy Songs* Lomax gives a similar text as "The Happy Miner," again without a tune. John Norman of Munising, Michigan, recorded it as "The Raving Shanty Boy" for the Library of Congress in 1938. All of these versions obviously sprang from the same source, probably a vaudeville song, but O. J. Abbott's is localized in the Canadian northwoods: the valley of the Gatineau River north of Ottawa, a famous lumbering region in the last century. His first stanza and refrain are like the other versions; the last two stanzas are quite different except for the line "Head and tail up like a steer running through the corn." He sings it to a popular square-dance tune usually known as "The Crooked Stovepipe."

REFERENCES

PRINTED. E. C. Beck, *Lore*, 11 (reprinted in E. C. Beck, *Bunyan*, 31–32). Lomax and Lomax, *Cowboy Songs*, 409–410.

RECORDED. Library of Congress AFS 2355A (John Norman). Prestige/International 25014 (Abbott, "The Jolly Shantyboy").

TUNE RELATIVES

Leach, 280. Peacock, 515.

55. My Jolly Shantyboy

Sung by Michael Cuddihey
Low, Quebec   August 1957

1. As I went out a-walking in the merry month of May,
   I spied a pretty fair maid, so charming she did say:
   "It's cruel are my parents, they do me so annoy,
   And they will not let me ramble with my jolly shantyboy."

Refrain

For his cheeks are like the roses, and he always wears good clothes.
He is admired by all the girls no matter where he goes.
He is so young and gentle, and his life he does enjoy.
If I had my will I'd love him still, my jolly shantyboy.

2. "Oh, daughter, dearest daughter, oh hold your foolish tongue,
Thinking to get married, sure you're altogether wrong.
Some drygoods clerk would suit you better, whose salary you'd enjoy,
Than to throw yourself away with a reckless shantyboy."

This is a lumbering version of the Irish song "The Bonny Laboring Boy" (M 14), which was also popular in the camps and which inspired another local variant, "The Railroad Boy." "My Jolly Shantyboy" has some strength in tradition: P. J. Thomas of Vancouver has recorded it from Mr. Fred Thompson of Hiffley Creek, British Columbia, who learned it in northern Ontario in about 1922.

Michael Cuddihey's tune is a variant of "The Boston Burglar."

References

recorded. National Museum FO 3-29 (Cuddihey).

For "The Bonny Laboring Boy" see Laws, *ABBB*, 187, and Dean-Smith, 54. For "The Railroad Boy" see Fowke and Mills, 200–201 and Folkways FM 4005 (Martin Sullivan).

Tune Relatives

Brown IV, 281–282. Fowke and Mills, 200–201. Leach, 254. Peacock, 869. Folkways FM 4051 (I–8).

56. No, My Boy, Not I

Sung by O. J. Abbott
Hull, Quebec October 1959

1. As I roved out one evening, as I roved out one day,
   I met a handsome lady by chance upon my way.
   I says, "My lovely damsel, won't you marry me by and by?"
   The answer that she made to me was, "No, my boy, not I.

2. "If I was to marry you, my boy, who'd be to blame?
   My friends and my relations would look on me with shame.
   You are of a low degree, and I am of so high,
   To think that I would marry you—oh, no, my boy, not I!"

3. I went to her house another night this fair maid to see.
   Before this night was over she grew very fond of me.
   I hugged her and I kissed her and I caused her for to sigh.
   She soon forgot the time she said, "Oh, no, my boy, not I."

4. Six months was passed and over, six months was passed and gone.
This beautiful and fair maid began to fret and frown.
She wrote me a letter: "Won't you marry me by and by?"
The answer that I made to her was, "No, my girl, not I.

5. "If I was to marry you, my girl, who'd be to blame?
My friends and my relations would look on me with shame.
You are of a low degree, and I am of so high,
To think that I would marry you—oh, no, my girl, not I.

6. "So now my dearest damsel, I'll tell you what to do:
Take the libby lad on your back and paddle your own canoe,
And when the day is over, you may sit down and cry,
And think upon the time you said, 'Oh, no, my boy, not I.' "

7. So come all you pretty damsels, a warning take by me:
Don't never let a shantyboy an inch above your knee,
For if you do he'll ruin you, he'll cause you for to cry.
He'll make you sing that little song, "Rock a baby *bye*."

"No, My Boy, Not I" is a neat localizing of a popular British ballad that appeared on many nineteenth-century broadsides as "O No, My Love, Not I." Leslie Shepard has located several broadside copies, the oldest of which, labeled "Pitts, Printer, and Toy Warehouse, Great St. Andrew Street 7 Dials," probably dates from the 1820's. The only British text reported from tradition was noted by Cecil Sharp in 1904. On this continent Leach found a slightly shorter version in Labrador, and Peacock found one beginning "A Newfoundland sailor was walking the strand."

All traditional texts are fairly similar to the broadsides. O. J. Abbott's last stanza, however, may have been transferred from another song. The shantyboys are probably responsible for advising the girl to "paddle her own canoe"; the British texts told her to "take your baby on your back and a-begging for to go." Joe Thibadeau sings a version closer to the British form.

The tune, the one Mr. Abbott used for "The Gatineau Girls," is more modern than the text.

REFERENCES

PRINTED. Leach, 280. Peacock, 304–305. Reeves, 108. Broadsides: Henderson, 79; J. Harkness, Preston, England (c. 1845); Walker, Durham, England; Pitts, London (c. 1819–1844).

TUNE RELATIVES. See Song 54.

57. The Roving Shantyboy

Sung by LaRena Clark
Ottawa, Ontario May 1965

1. Come all you true-born shantyboys wherever you may be,
   Come fill up your flowing bowls when in good company.
   Don't use the least resistance or fortune may prove shy.
   Bring wine to your assistance like a roving shantyboy.

2. And when I meet a pretty fair maid when in good company
   I've just enough of impert'ence to take her on my knee.
   I'd talk of love and rapture, and I would make her sigh.
   I'd say, "My dove, why can't you love this roving shantyboy?"

3. And she'd become more comical, and eagerly I'd press
   With something more than modesty, to this I must confess.
   I courted her on winter's nights; with me she did comply.
   Then I was away by the first of May like a roving shantyboy.

4. "Oh, now he's gone and left me, he cared not for to break.
The corner of my handkerchief contains my whole estate.
He courted me on winter's nights; with him I did comply.
Then he was away by the first of May like a roving shantyboy.

5. "Oh, now he's gone and left me, his vows they are all broke
[they all did break].
My parents ofttimes told me they thought he was a rake,
And now for satisfaction I may sit down and sigh,
And whisper in my baby's ear, 'Your daddy's a shantyboy.' "

Like "No, My Boy, Not I," this song emphasizes the amorous adventures of the shantyboys. It also is probably adapted from an older British song, but here the original has proved harder to identify. LaRena Clark learned the song from her grandfather Watson, who was of English ancestry. It was first printed in my *More Folk Songs of Canada* (pp. 88–89).

TUNE RELATIVES

Barry, 28. Bayard, 38–39. Cazden, *Abelard* I, 42. Creighton and Senior, 221. Joyce, *OIFM*, no. 600. Leach, 100. O'Lochlainn, 50, 88. Peacock, 204. Petrie, nos. 704, 753, 1191.

58. The Jolly Raftsman O

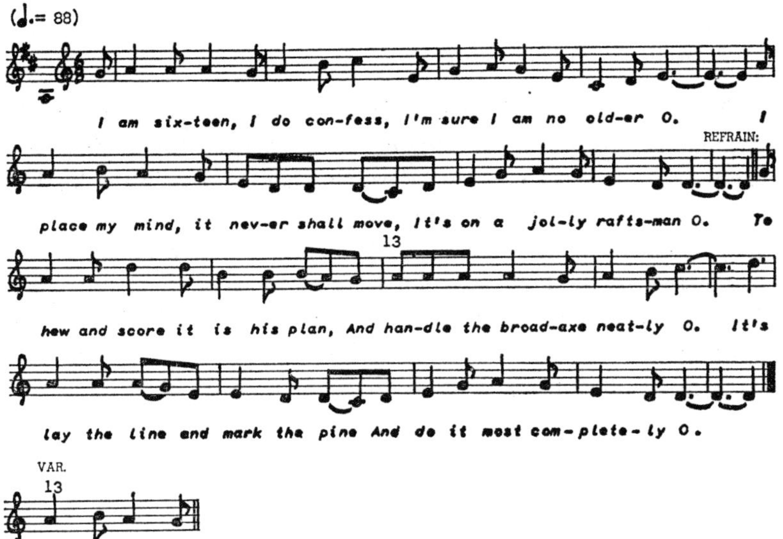

Sung by Grace Fraser
Lancaster, Ontario   September 1961

1. I am sixteen, I do confess,
   I'm sure I am no older O.
   I place my mind, it never shall move,
   It's on a jolly raftsman O.

REFRAIN
   To hew and score it is his plan,
   And handle the broadaxe neatly O.
   It's lay the line and mark the pine
   And do it most completely O.

2. Oh, she is daily scolding me
   To marry some freeholder O.
   I place my mind, it never shall move,
   It's on a jolly raftsman O.

3. My love is marching through the pine
   As brave as Alexander O
   And none can I find to please my mind
   As well as a jolly raftsman O.

This beautiful little love lyric is quite different from any of the other lumbering songs. Mrs. Fraser learned it from her mother, who may have learned it from her father, who had worked in the lumber-camps. The tune probably comes from the Scottish Highlands, although Norman Cazden finds resemblances to "The Drunken Sailor," "Pat Works on the Railway," and a New Brunswick version of "The Heights of Alma" (Manny, p. 247). The song was first printed in my *Traditional Singers and Songs from Ontario* (pp. 78–79), and Mrs. Fraser may be heard singing it on Prestige/International 25014.

L' ENVOI

59. I Am a River Driver

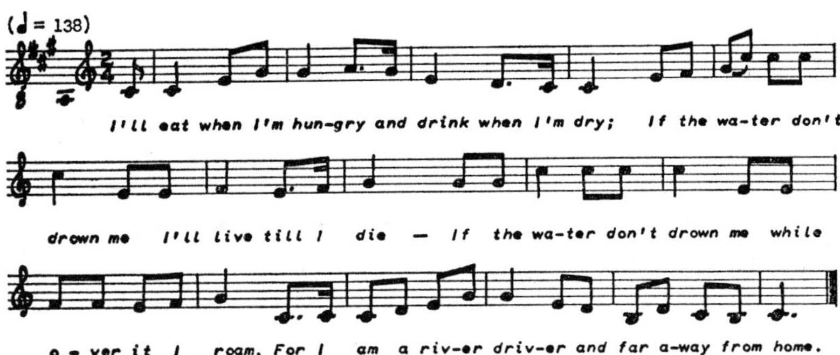

Sung by John Leahy
Douro, Ontario November 1958

I'll eat when I'm hungry and drink when I'm dry;
If the water don't drown me I'll live till I die—
If the water don't drown me while over it I roam,
For I am a river driver and far away from home.

This fragment was all John Leahy could remember of a rather rare song reported only from Maine and Newfoundland. The hero of the Maine version worked six months on the drive before reaching Quebec, where he met his Molly. The song obviously descended from the same British song as "Jack of Diamonds," "Rye Whiskey," and "The Rebel Soldier." Kittredge identified this ancestor as "The Forsaken Girl." The tune has been used for a Pennsylvania miners' song, "Down, Down, Down."

References

PRINTED. Eckstorm, 61–62. Peacock, 759–760. For a note on related songs, see Cox, 279.

Tune Relatives

Kidson, 100. Korson, 364.

60. Driving Saw-Logs on the Plover (dC 29)

Sung by Bob McMahon
Peterborough, Ontario October 1959

1. The river flowed her mighty banks one evening last July.
   The mother of a shantyboy, and doleful was her cry,
   Saying, "God be with you, Johnny, although you're far away,
   To drive saw-logs on the Plover, and you'll never get your pay.

2. "Johnny, I gave you schoolin', and I gave you a trade likewise.
   You need not be a shantyman if you'd taken my advice.
   You need not roam from your dear home to the forest far away
   For to drive the lonesome river, and you'll never get your pay.

3. "Oh, you'd be better to stay up on the farm and feed the ducks and hens,
   To drive the sheep and pigs each night and put them in their pens.
   Far better for you to help your dad a-cut his corn and hay
   Than to drive those logs on the Plover, and you'll never get your pay."

4. So an old canoe came floating all on the quiet stream,
   And peacefully it glided like some young lover's dream.
   A youth crept out upon the banks, and this to her did say:
   "Oh, mother dear, I jumped the job and never got my pay.
5. "Now the boys called me a sucker and a son of a gun to boot.
   I said to myself, now Johnny, it's time for you to scoot,
   So I stole a canoe and I started all on my merry way,
   And now I am at home again and nary a cent of pay."
6. So all young men take this advice before you leave your home:
   Be sure you kiss your mother before you leave your home.
   Far better for you upon the farm for half a dollar a day
   Than to drive the lonesome river, and you'll never get your pay.

Rickaby gives the only previous text of this ballad. He got it from the author, Mr. W. N. Allen, who headed it "A Doleful Ditty, by Shan T. Boy." Rickaby says it was composed in 1873 and had some currency in Wisconsin, though it never won the popularity of Mr. Allen's other song, "The Banks of the Little Eau Pleine." The Plover, like the Little Eau Pleine, is a tributary of the Wisconsin River. These verses were obviously inspired by a British broadside, "The Crimean War" (J 9), which also features a conversation between a mother and son.

Bob McMahon's tune, similar to the one Rickaby gives, is Irish and has been used for many songs in both Ireland and North America.

REFERENCES

PRINTED. Laws, *NAB*, 261 (Rickaby, 89–91; reprinted in Carmer, 173–174, and Sandburg, 396–397).

RECORDED. National Museum, FO 19-181 (McMahon).

Cf. "The Crimean War," Laws, *ABBB*, 132–133.

TUNE RELATIVES

Brown IV, 341. Creighton and Senior, 78. Doerflinger, 113, 222. Edwards, 29. Fowke and Mills, 92. Galvin, 50. Gardner, 231, 261, 399. Grainger, no. 239. Ives, *NEF* 5 (1963), 15. Joyce, *OIFM*, nos. 13, 624. Leach, 186, 198. Manny, 82, 122, 140. Peacock, 620, 942. Randolph I, 32, 36. Rickaby, 89. Wilson, 21–22 (nos. 11 and 11a–11e), 43 nn.

61. Save Your Money While You're Young

Sung by Jim Doherty
Peterborough, Ontario June 1957

1. Come all you jolly good fellows, I'll sing to you a song.
   It's all about the shantyboys and it won't take me long,
   For it's now that I regret the day while I'm working out in the cold—
   Save your money while you're young, my boys, you'll need it when you're old.

2. For once I was a shantyboy, oh, wasn't I a lad!
   Now the way I spent my money, oh, wasn't it too bad!
   For it's now that I regret the day while I'm working out in the cold—
   Save your money while you're young, my boys, you'll need it when you're old.

3. And if you are a married man, I'll tell you what to do:
   Just be good to your wife and family as you were sworn to do.

Keep away from all grog shops, where liquor is bought and sold—
Save your money while you're young, my boys, you'll need it when you're old.

4. And if you are a single man, I'll tell you what to do:
Just court some pretty girl that to you will prove true.
Just court some pretty girl that is not overbold,
That will stick to you through life and be a comfort when you're old.

5. For once I was a shantyboy, oh, wasn't I a lad!
Now the way I spent my money, oh, wasn't it too bad!
For it's now that I regret the day while I'm working out in the cold—
Save your money while you're young, my boys, you'll need it when you're old.

This melancholy postscript to the shantyboy's life is quite rare: only three other versions have been reported. Jim Doherty's tune differs from Rickaby's, the only other one noted for this song, but is similar to that of "Young Conway," used for many Irish and American songs.

REFERENCES

PRINTED. E. C. Beck, *Lore*, 95. Finger, 138–139. Fowke, 134–135 (same as above). Rickaby, 39–40.

RECORDED. Folkways FM 4052 (Doherty).

TUNE RELATIVES. See Song 42.

62. You Can't Keep a Shantyboy Down

Sung by Ron Sisson
West Guilford, Ontario May 1965

1. Kind friends, your attention I'll ask for awhile,
   A few facts I endeavor to show.
   This world is a network that's wove very small:
   'Twill snare you as through life we go.
   With troubles and toils we all have our share;
   That's the way wealthy men gain renown,
   And the way that you show it I'll now tell to you,
   For you can't keep a shantyboy down.

2. A shantyboy works, his money he spends
With his comrades so happy and gay,
And scarce the week has come to an end
When his wages have all passed away.
Where if he laid by a dollar or two
And placed it in some bank in town,
He could now wink at his boss on the sly,
For you can't keep a shantyboy down.

3. So take this old building, it stands here tonight;
Compare it, for this is my plan.
The roof is aristocracy, so are the walls,
Foundation's the hard-working man.
Go tear off the roof. The walls will remain.
Look at the foundation still strong.
Tear away the foundation the workingman's laid,
And the structure will fall to the ground.

4. Then hold up your head, this world never dread.
Care not for a sneer or a frown.
Stare fate in the face, if your heart's in its place,
For you can't keep a shantyboy down.

(The fragmentary last stanza is sung to the second half of the tune.)

Ron Sisson learned this song from his mother and believes that she learned it from some of the shantyboys who worked in the mill near his home in West Guilford. It is obviously an adaptation of an English song about "The Hard-Working Man," as the third stanza shows. The tune is of popular rather than folk origin.

63. The Kipawa Stream

(To the tune of Song 52.)

Sung by Lloyd Gavan
Quyon, Quebec November 1966

1. I am a roving shantyboy—the pinewoods is my home.
   Like every other fellow, from camp to camp I roam,
   And many a foaming river goes throughout the foreign land.
   I'm now upon the Kipawa with a peavey in my hand.

2. I've been a jolly lumberman for seven long years or more;
   I could run those noisy rapids where the foaming billows roar.
   I could enjoy all kinds of pleasure: I could whistle, dance, and sing;
   I could make the taverns echo and could make those ballrooms ring.

3. My muscle is my fortune; it's hard work I don't fear,
   And the money that I'm earning now will never go for beer.
   I'll save it up in store, my boys, until I'm older grown,
   And then I'll marry some pretty young girl and no more roving go.

4. It's on the old Muskegon, boy, where many a dollar I earned;
   From Michigan to the Kipawa each bar and crook I learned.
   The men of steel assembled a butterfly so grand;
   I'm on the Mississagi now with my peavey in my hand.

5. It's once for cash a-plenty and now for money bare,
   But while we've got the coppers, boys, to spend them we don't spare.
   With a pretty young girl upon my knee and a bottle in my right hand,
   We'll drink success to the riverboy and a health to Paddy's land.

6. We take our morning bitters in the morning when we rise,
   And a couple or more will help us to open up our eyes.
   We fear no kind of danger while in our birch canoe:
   We could run those noisy rapids and the cellars of Long Sault.

7. If British laws they would allow, it's great revenge I'd take.
   I'd cause those Indians' heads to ring and their hearts all for to break.
   I'd cause those Indians' heads to ring and their hearts all for to break.
   With guns, canoes, and paddles, boys, we ofttimes *roved the lakes.*

Though this is one of the better examples of the shantyboys' rhyming skill, Lloyd and Lennox Gavan are the only singers I have found who know it. It is obviously inspired by "The Boardman River Song" known in Michigan. E. C. Beck notes that another version, "The Manistee River Song," was said to have been composed by Ole Nelson of Sherman in 1880. Alan Lomax recorded another Michigan version for the Library of Congress as "The Roving Lumberjack."

Stanzas 1, 3, and 4 of the Canadian song are very close to the text Beck gives, except that the Boardman has become the Kipawa, a Quebec river that drains into the Ottawa near Timiskaming. (For an interesting example of oral change, note how "On the Manistee and Butterfield" becomes "the men of steel assembled a butterfly so grand" —a poetic description of a high steel bridge.) The other four stanzas are quite different and were probably composed in Canada.

The tune, a popular one in the lumberwoods, is used in Ontario for "The Farmer's Son and the Shantyboy."

REFERENCES

PRINTED. E. C. Beck, *Lore*, 55–57.
RECORDED. Library of Congress AFS 2260 (Bill McBride).

TUNE RELATIVES. See Song 52.

64. The Raftsmen's Song

Sung by LaRena Clark
Ottawa, Ontario August 1965

1. I believe some dust of the wanderlust has been molded with my clay.
   Though I long to come to my home sweet home, it's never long I'll stay.
   Perhaps a surge of the water's urge from the Laurentides to the sea
   That stirs the flood of the rover's blood in old waterdogs like me.
   So I long to go back to the Pontiac, to the river where the rafts flow through,
   To wend my way to the Dutchman's Bay and along the Roche Fondue,
   To camp at the foot of the mountain chute where in fancy I heard the strain
   Of the raftsmen's song as they swept along, a-singing their bold refrain:

REFRAIN

Now row, boys, row, through the channel we will go
With a heave and a ho, hi, ho.
Now row, boys, row, shoot the rapids down below
With a heave and a ho, hi, ho.

2. There are raftsmen's bones 'neath cairns of stone where the foam-white waters toss,
   And many a mound where the rapids sound have been marked with a pine or cross,
   For grim death stalks where the treacherous rocks have thrust from the channel's bed,
   And many who set out with a hail and a shout have come down the cascades dead.
   Oh, the Calumet crags and the Dargy snags and the reef where the Sable flings,

And the Iroquois Nose and the Devil's Toes, and the Tooths and the Three Great Kings,
And woe betide if it swings too wide at the portage bridge's pier:
They would crash on the rocks with a shuddering shock that would chill your blood with fear.

3. Those old raftsmen who were singing then, they are scattered far today.
No more they'll ride Carmichael's slide or plunge into Roche Manay.
No more they'll go by the Devil's Bow in their roaring, reckless scorn;
No more they'll try for the lazy snye or swing around Cape Horn.
When word comes through for a timber crew for the river beyond the skies,
They'll ride the slide through the Great Divide, coming clear into heaven's snyes.
Those old raftsmen will be happy then with the Lord to pay their fee
As they sing their song as they sail along on the river of eternity.

This unusual song, which LaRena Clark learned from her father, does not seem to be known by any other singer. Its idiom is so different from all the other lumbering songs that I suspect it was written by a minor Canadian poet rather than a shantyboy, but I have failed to trace the author. Whoever he was, he must have known the waterways of the northern woods at first hand, for he has made effective use of local place names and described the river hazards most graphically. The unusual word *snye* in the last stanza is a lumberman's term for a side channel in the river and comes from the Canadian French *chenail*, meaning channel. Sable River lies north of Manitoulin Island, Calumet Island is in the Ottawa River just east of Pembroke, and the Laurentides may be found north of the city of Quebec. The imagery of the last four lines recalls the familiar cowboy songs that describe "the last round-up in the sky." The tune is based on the second part of "O Susanna."

65. The Opeongo Line

On the Opeongo Line
I drove a span of bays
One summer once upon a time
For Hoolihan and Hayes.
Now that the bays are dead and gone
And grim old age is mine,
A phantom team and teamster start
From Renfrew, rain or shine—

Aye, dreaming, dreaming, I go teaming
On the Opeongo Line.

Fragment collected by the Reverend Joseph E. Gravelle, Otter Lake, Quebec. Author and tune unknown.

NOTES ON THE SINGERS

Thirty-four different singers are represented in this book, and the baker's dozen described below have each contributed three or more songs. Their backgrounds are remarkably similar—most are of Irish descent, most are farmers who spent many winters in the woods, and most know many other songs besides the ones given here. Seven of them are featured in *Traditional Singers and Songs from Ontario*, where more detailed biographical notes are given.

O. J. Abbott was an exceptionally fine traditional singer with an extensive repertory. Born in England in 1872, he came to Canada as a boy of twelve. He worked on farms in an Irish community in the Ottawa Valley and learned numerous songs from the farmers' sons, many of whom went shantying in the winter. Mr. Abbott himself worked in the lumbercamps for five seasons in the 1890's before he moved into Hull. He was eighty-five when I first met him but still remembered perfectly the songs he had learned some sixty years earlier. Some of his songs are on Folkways FM 4051 and other records. He died in 1962.

Tom Brandon, born in Midland, Ontario, in 1927, grew up in Kinmount, where his father worked in a lumber mill. At sixteen Tom began working on the boats on the Great Lakes in summer and in the lumbercamps in winter, continuing this routine for nine years. In 1951 he took a job with the Canadian Pacific Railway in Toronto, moving to Peterborough six years later. He has made a record for Folk Legacy (FSC 10) and has appeared at the Mariposa and Philadelphia Folk Festivals.

Mrs. Gordon Clark, born LaRena LeBarre, has an unusual background. The LeBarres were originally French colonists who came to Acadia early in the eighteenth century. Her grandfather obtained a land grant on Lake Simcoe, where LaRena was born in 1917. LaRena's father and grandfather were hunters and guides, working in the woods of northern Ontario, and she learned most of her songs from them. She has a record on the Topic label (12T140).

Michael Cuddihey, born in 1888, has farmed all his life and spent many winters in the lumbercamps of northern Ontario. When I first met him he was living just outside the village of Low, some thirty miles north of Ottawa. His Grandfather Cuddihey came over from Kilkenny, and many other families around Low are of Irish descent. In 1964 Mr. Cuddihey moved to Hull, where he now lives with his son.

Jim Doherty was born on his father's farm near Otonabee in 1893. His grandparents on both sides came from Ireland. He went to work in the lumbercamps during the First World War, and later farmed at Otonabee. He worked for Canadian General Electric in Peterborough for many years before he retired in 1961.

Lennox Gavan runs Gavan's Hotel in the village of Quyon on the north shore of the Ottawa River some thirty miles west of Ottawa. A fine singer, he performs at local functions and has also appeared on country-music television shows and at the Mariposa Folk Festival. Both he and his brother Lloyd learned some unusual songs from their mother, although now they usually sing more common Irish numbers.

George McCallum was born in 1881, and when I visited him in 1961 he was still running his own farm near Grafton, some seventy miles east of Toronto. In his younger days he had spent many winters in the lumbercamps up north and had picked up unusual songs as well as well-known ones. He sang many good tunes for me, and despite his age his voice was strong and clear.

Dave McMahon was born in 1903 in Otonobee township and grew up on a farm in neighboring Douro township near Peterborough. His grandfathers on both sides of his family came from Ireland. He first went to the lumberwoods the winter he was seventeen, and went back each year until he was twenty-five. Since his marriage in 1935 he has farmed near the village of Douro, some ten miles east of Peterborough. His younger brother, Bob McMahon, has a farm just across the road.

Ron Sisson, who lives in West Guilford, a Haliburton village, is considerably younger than most of the other singers: he was thirty-seven when I recorded him in 1965. He had learned some songs from his mother, and when he worked for Hay and Company some sixteen years earlier he composed a couple that are very much like the typical lumbercamp "moniker" ditties.

Leo Spencer is a farmer at Lakefield, ten miles north of Peterborough. His father came from Ireland to settle in South Burleigh, where he became a lumberman. Leo was born there in 1892, and when he was old enough he worked for his father in the woods for five winters. Then between 1917 and 1923 he went to work in the northern camps. In 1901 his father bought a farm near Lakefield, and Leo took over the farm when his father died in 1924.

Martin Sullivan is the son of the "old Tom Sullivan" who figures in many fine yarns told around the Peterborough district. His brother, Tom Sullivan of Lakefield, is a good fiddler, and his two sisters, Miss Maggie Sullivan and Mrs. Tom O'Brien of Peterborough, have both sung for me. Martin spent many winters in the lumbercamps, and when I met him he was working on a farm near Nassau, a few miles north of Peterborough.

Joe Thibadeau, who was seventy-six when I met him in 1964, has a remarkable stock of songs and tall tales. Despite his French name, he says his father was Scottish, born in St. John, New Brunswick. His mother was from New York state. After his father died at thirty-eight, his mother married again, and the nine boys had to get out to work. Joe went to work in the woods when he was thirteen. He spent quite a few years in the Lake of the Woods and Rainy River district, and then settled in Bobcaygeon, a pretty little town some thirty miles northwest of Peterborough. For over twenty-five years he has been a licensed guide, and his tales of the days when he worked for Paul Bunyan have entertained hundreds of tourists.

Emerson Woodcock was born on a farm near Kinmount in 1899 and began working in the lumberwoods when he was fourteen. From 1913 to 1921 he spent every winter in the woods. Next he worked in lumber mills around Kinmount for six years, and in 1927 moved to Peterborough, where he worked for the General Electric Company until he retired in 1964.

BIBLIOGRAPHY

PRINTED MATERIAL

Barry, Phillips. *The Maine Woods Songster*. Cambridge: Harvard University Press, 1939.

Bayard, Samuel P. "Folk Tunes from the Phillips Barry Collection," 1942. Transcribed from dictaphone recordings. MS at Widener Library, Harvard University, #27256.155.193.

Beck, Earl Clifton. *Lore of the Lumber Camps*. Ann Arbor: University of Michigan Press, 1948.

———. *They Knew Paul Bunyan*. Ann Arbor: University of Michigan Press, 1956.

Beck, Horace P. *The Folklore of Maine*. Philadelphia and New York: J. B. Lippincott Co., 1957.

Bedore, Bernie. "The Haggarty Boys and Young Mulvannon." *Renfrew Advance*, November 14, 1963, p. 4.

Belden, Henry Marvin. *Ballads and Songs Collected by the Missouri Folk-Lore Society*. The University of Missouri Studies, vol. 15, no. 1. Columbia, 1940; reprinted 1955.

Broadwood, Lucy, and J. A. Fuller Maitland. *English County Songs*. London: The Leadenhall Press, 1893.

Bronson, Bertrand Harris. *The Traditional Tunes of the Child Ballads*. Vol. 1. Princeton, New Jersey: Princeton University Press, 1959.

Brown, Frank C. *The Frank C. Brown Collection of North Carolina Folklore*. 7 vols. Gen. ed. Newman Ivey White. Durham, North Carolina: Duke University Press, 1952–1964.

Bulletin of the Folk-Song Society of the Northeast. Nos. 1–12. Cambridge, Massachusetts, 1930–1937.

Campbell, Thomas J. "The Farmer's Son and the Shanty Boy." *Word-Lore* 1:6 (1926), 222–223.

Carmer, Carl. *Songs of the Rivers of America.* New York: Farrar and Rinehart, 1942.

Cazden, Norman. *The Abelard Folk Song Book.* New York: Abelard-Schuman, 1958.

———. "Catskill Lockup Songs." *New York Folklore Quarterly* 16 (1960), 90–103.

———. "Regional and Occupational Orientations to American Traditional Song." *Journal of American Folklore* 72 (1959), 310–344.

Checklist of Recorded Songs in the English Language in the Archive of American Folk Song to July, 1940. Washington, D.C.: The Library of Congress, Music Division, 1942.

Colcord, Joanna C. *Songs of American Sailormen.* New York: W. W. Norton, 1938.

Cox, John Harrington. *Folksongs of the South.* Cambridge: Harvard University Press, 1925.

Creighton, Helen. *Maritime Folk Songs.* Toronto: Ryerson Press, 1962.

———. *Songs and Ballads from Nova Scotia.* Toronto and Vancouver: J. M. Dent, 1933.

———, and Doreen Senior. *Traditional Songs from Nova Scotia.* Toronto: Ryerson Press, 1950.

Dean, Michael C. *The Flying Cloud and One Hundred and Fifty Other Old Time Songs and Ballads.* Virginia, Minnesota: The Quickprint, 1922.

Dean-Smith, Margaret. *A Guide to English Folk Song Collections, 1822–1952.* Published in association with the English Folk Dance and Song Society. Liverpool: The University Press of Liverpool, 1954.

Doerflinger, William Main. *Shantymen and Shantyboys: Songs of the Sailor and Lumberman.* New York: The Macmillan Co., 1951.

Dorson, Richard M. *Buying the Wind.* Chicago and London: University of Chicago Press, 1964.

———. "Folksongs of the Maine Woods." *Folklore and Folk Music Archivist* 8:1 (1966), 3–33.

Doyle, Gerald S. *Old-Time Songs of Newfoundland.* St. John's, Newfoundland: Gerald S. Doyle Ltd., 1955.

Eckstorm, Fannie Hardy, and Mary Winslow Smyth. *Minstrelsy of Maine.* Boston and New York: Houghton, Mifflin Co., 1927.

Edwards, R. F. *The Overlander Songbook.* Victoria, Australia: The Rams Skull Press, 1956.

Finger, Charles J. *Frontier Ballads.* New York: Doubleday, Page and Co., 1927.

Flanders, Helen Hartness. *A Garland of Green Mountain Song.* Green Mountain Pamphlets, no. 1. Northfield, Vermont, 1934.

———, Elizabeth Flanders Ballard, George Brown, and Phillips Barry. *The New Green Mountain Songster: Traditional Folksongs of Vermont.* New Haven, Connecticut: Yale University Press, 1939.

———, and George Brown. *Vermont Folk-Songs and Ballads.* Brattleboro, Vermont: Stephen Daye Press, 1931.

———, and Marguerite Olney. *Ballads Migrant in New England.* New York: Farrar, Straus, and Young, 1953.

Fowke, Edith. *Traditional Singers and Songs from Ontario.* Hatboro, Pennsylvania: Folklore Associates; Don Mills, Ontario: Burns & MacEachern, 1965.

———, and Richard Johnston. *More Folk Songs of Canada.* Waterloo, Ontario: Waterloo Music Company Ltd., 1967.

———, and Alan Mills. *Canada's Story in Song.* Toronto: W. J. Gage Ltd., 1960.

Galvin, Patrick. *Irish Songs of Resistance.* New York: Folklore Press, n.d.

Gard, Robert E., and L. A. Gordon. *Wisconsin Lore.* New York: Duell, Sloan & Pearce, 1962.

Gardner, Emelyn Elizabeth, and Geraldine J. Chickering. *Ballads and Songs of Southern Michigan.* Ann Arbor: University of Michigan Press, 1939.

Gordon, Robert Winslow. Manuscript collection in the Archive of American Folk Song. Library of Congress, Washington, D.C.

Grainger, Percy, and Rose Grainger. Collection of English folksongs, sea chanties, etc. Hektographed, 1907. New York Public Library, Music Division.

Gravelle, Jos. E. "The Drowning of Jimmy Judge." *Renfrew Advance,* September 29, 1966.

Gray, Roland Palmer. *Songs and Ballads of the Maine Lumberjacks.* Cambridge, Massachusetts: Harvard University Press, 1924.

Greenleaf, Elisabeth Bristol, and Grace Mansfield. *Ballads and Sea Songs from Newfoundland.* Cambridge, Massachusetts: Harvard University Press, 1933.

Greig, Gavin. *Folk-Song of the North-East.* Articles in the *Buchan Ob-*

server, December 1907 to June 1911. Hatboro, Pennsylvania: Folklore Associates, 1963.

Grover, Carrie B. *A Heritage of Songs.* Privately printed, n.p., n.d.

Harlow, Frederick Pease. *Chanteying Aboard American Ships.* Barre, Massachusetts: Barre Gazette, 1962.

Henderson, W. *Victorian Street Ballads.* London and New York: Charles Scribner's Sons, 1938.

Henry, Sam. "Songs of the People." A manuscript and newspaper-clipping collection of songs collected for the *Northern Constitution* of Coleraine, Ireland, between 1923 and 1939.

Holbrook, Stewart H. *Holy Old Mackinaw.* New York: Macmillan, 1938.

Hubbard, Lester A. *Ballads and Songs from Utah.* Salt Lake City: The University of Utah Press, 1961.

Hughes, Herbert. *Irish Country Songs.* 4 vols. London: Boosey & Hawkes, 1909.

Hugill, Stan. *Shanties from the Seven Seas.* New York and London: E. P. Dutton, 1961.

Ives, Edward D. "Folksongs from Maine." *Northeast Folklore* 7 (1965), 1–104.

———. *Larry Gorman, the Man Who Made the Songs.* Bloomington: Indiana University Press, 1964.

———. "The Lumberman in Town." *Northeast Folklore* 2:4 (1959), 58–59.

———. "Twenty-one Folksongs from Prince Edward Island." *Northeast Folklore* 5 (1963), 1–87.

Jackson, Bruce. *Folklore & Society: Essays in Honor of Benj. A. Botkin.* Hatboro, Pennsylvania: Folklore Associates, 1966.

Joyce, Patrick W. *Ancient Irish Music.* Dublin: Longmans Green and Co., 1912.

———. *Old Irish Folk Music and Song.* Dublin: Hodges, Figgis & Co., 1909.

Kaiser, Robert A. "Lumberman's Ballad, 'Shannel's Mill.' " *New York Folklore Quarterly* 11 (1955), 133–135.

Kidson, Frank. *Traditional Tunes.* Oxford: Chas. Taphouse and Son, 1891.

Korson, George. *Pennsylvania Songs and Legends.* Philadelphia: University of Pennsylvania Press, 1949.

Laws, G. Malcolm, Jr. *American Balladry from British Broadsides: A Guide for Students and Collectors of Traditional Song.* Publications of the

American Folklore Society, Bibliographical and Special Series, Vol. 8. Philadelphia, 1957.

———. *Native American Balladry: A Descriptive Study and a Bibliographical Syllabus*. Publications of the American Folklore Society, Bibliographical and Special Series, Vol. 1, rev. ed. Philadelphia, 1964.

Leach, MacEdward. *Folk Ballads and Songs of the Lower Labrador Coast*. Ottawa: The National Museum of Canada, 1965.

Linscott, Eloise Hubbard. *Folk Songs of Old New England*. New York: Macmillan, 1939.

Lloyd, A. L. *Come All Ye Bold Miners: Ballads & Songs of the Coalfields*. London: Lawrence & Wishart Ltd., 1952.

Lomax, Alan. *The Folk Songs of North America*. Garden City, New York: Doubleday and Co., 1960.

Lomax, John, and Alan Lomax. *American Ballads and Folk Songs*. New York: Macmillan, 1934.

———. *Cowboy Songs and Other Frontier Ballads*. New York: Macmillan, 1925.

———. *Folk Song U.S.A.* New York: Duell, Sloan & Pearce, 1947.

———. *Our Singing Country*. New York: Macmillan, 1951.

Mackenzie, W. Roy. *Ballads and Sea Songs from Nova Scotia*. Cambridge, Massachusetts: Harvard University Press, 1928.

Manny, Louise, and James Reginald Wilson. *Songs of Miramichi*. Fredericton, New Brunswick: Brunswick Press, 1968.

Moore, Ethel, and Chauncey O. Moore. *Ballads and Folk Songs of the Southwest*. Norman: University of Oklahoma Press, 1964.

Morris, Alton C. *Folksongs of Florida*. Gainesville: University of Florida Press, 1950.

O'Lochlainn, Colm. *Irish Street Ballads*. Dublin: The Sign of the Three Candles, 1939.

O'Neill, Capt. Francis. *O'Neill's Music of Ireland*. Chicago: Lyon & Healy, 1903.

Peacock, Kenneth. *Songs of the Newfoundland Outports*. 3 vols. Ottawa: National Museum of Canada, 1965.

Petrie, George. *Complete Collection of Irish Music*. Ed. Charles Villiers Stanford. London: Boosey & Co., 1902–1905.

Pike, Robert E. "Folk Songs from Pittsburgh, New Hampshire." *Journal of American Folklore* 48 (1935), 337–351.

Pound, Louise. *American Ballads and Songs*. New York: Charles Scribner's Sons, 1922.

Randolph, Vance. *Ozark Folksongs*. 4 vols. Columbia: The State Historical Society of Missouri, 1946–1950.

Ranson, Joseph. *Songs of the Wexford Coast*. Enniscorthy: Redmond Bros., 1948.

Reeves, James. *The Idiom of the People: English Traditional Verse from the Manuscripts of Cecil J. Sharp*. London: William Heinemann, Ltd., 1958.

Rickaby, Franz. *Ballads and Songs of the Shanty-Boy*. Cambridge, Massachusetts: Harvard University Press, 1926.

Sandburg, Carl. *The American Songbag*. New York: Harcourt, Brace, & Co., 1927.

Sharp, Cecil J. *English Folk-Songs from the Southern Appalachians*. 2 vols. London: Oxford University Press, 1932.

Shoemaker, Henry W. *Mountain Minstrelsy of Pennsylvania*. Philadelphia: Newman F. McGirr, 1931.

Springer, John S. *Forest Life and Forest Trees*. New York: Harper & Row, 1851.

Thomas, Jean. *Ballad Makin' in the Mountains of Kentucky*. New York: Henry Holt and Co., 1939.

Thompson, Harold W. *Body, Boots, and Britches*. Philadelphia: Lippincott Co., 1939.

Thorp, N. Howard ("Jack"). *Songs of the Cowboys*. Eds. Austin E. Fife and Alta S. Fife. New York: Clarkson N. Potter, Inc., 1966.

Tolman, Albert H. "Traditional Texts and Tunes." *Journal of American Folklore* 35 (1922), 335–432.

Vincent, Elmore. *Lumberjack Songs*. Chicago: M. M. Cole, 1932.

Warner, Frank. *Folk Songs and Ballads of the Eastern Seaboard*. Macon, Georgia: Southern Press, Inc., 1963.

Waugh, F. W. "Canadian Folk-lore from Ontario." *Journal of American Folklore* 31 (1918), 4–82.

White, Stewart Edward. *The Blazed Trail*. New York: Grosset and Dunlap, 1902.

Wilson, James Reginald. "Ballad Tunes of the Miramichi." Master's thesis, New York University, 1961.

Wright, Dick. "Holmes Camp Song." *Spin* 3:9 (1965), 12–13.

RECORDINGS

Caedmon TC 1144. *Jack of All Trades*. Vol. 3 of *Folk Songs of Britain*. Collected and edited by Peter Kennedy and Alan Lomax.

——— TC 1145. *The Child Ballads*. Vol. 4 of *Folk Songs of Britain*.

E.F.D.S.S. LP 1003. *Pedlar's Pack*. Sung by John Doherty of Donegal. Recorded by Peter Kennedy. Issued by the English Folk Dance and Song Society.

Folk Legacy FSC 9. *Marie Hare of Strathadam, New Brunswick*.

——— FSC 10. *Tom Brandon of Peterborough, Ontario*.

——— FSA 15. *Lawrence Older of Middle Grove, New York*.

——— FSB 20. *Harry Cox Sings "Traditional English Love Songs."*

Folkways FA 2019. *Sea Shanties and Logging Songs*. Sung by Sam Eskin.

——— FA 2317. *Mountain Music of Kentucky*. Collected by John Cohen.

——— FA 2354. *Songs of a New York Lumberjack*. Sung by Ellen Stekert.

——— FG 3507. *Now is the Time for Fishing*. Sung by Sam Larner. Recorded by Ewan MacColl and Peggy Seeger.

——— FS 3809. *Fine Times at Our House: Traditional Music of Indiana*. Collected by Pat Dunford and Art Rosenbaum.

——— FM 4001. *Wolf River Songs*. Collected by Sidney Robertson Cowell.

——— FM 4005. *Folk Songs of Ontario*. Collected by Edith Fowke.

——— FM 4018. *Songs of the Great Lakes*. Collected by Edith Fowke.

——— FM 4051. *Irish and British Songs from the Ottawa Valley*. Sung by O. J. Abbott. Collected by Edith Fowke.

——— FM 4052. *Lumbering Songs from the Ontario Shanties*. Collected by Edith Fowke.

——— FM 4053. *Folksongs of the Miramichi*. Recorded at the Miramichi Folk Festival, Newcastle, New Brunswick.

——— FE 4075. *Songs from the Out-Ports of Newfoundland*. Collected by MacEdward Leach.

——— FE 4307. *Maritime Folk Songs*. Collected by Helen Creighton.

——— FE 4312. *Folksongs of Saskatchewan*. Collected by Barbara Cass-Beggs.

——— FH 5210. *Champlain Valley Songs*. From the Marjorie Porter collection. Sung by Pete Seeger.

——— FH 5273. *Tipple, Loom & Rail*. Sung by Mike Seeger.

——— FE 5323. *Folk Songs of Maine*. Sung by Sandy Ives.

——— FW 6821. *Folk Songs of the Canadian North Woods*. Sung by Wade Hemsworth.

Library of Congress AAFS L1. *Anglo-American Ballads*. Edited by Alan Lomax.

——— AAFS L28. *Cowboy Songs, Ballads, and Cattle Calls from Texas.* Edited by Duncan Emrich.

——— AAFS L55. *Folk Music from Wisconsin.* Edited by Helen Stratman-Thomas.

——— AAFS L56. *Songs of the Michigan Lumberjacks.* Edited by E. C. Beck.

Prestige/International 25014. *Ontario Ballads and Folksongs.* Collected by Edith Fowke.

Prestige/Irish 35001. *The Blarney Stone.* Sung by Margaret Barry.

Riverside RLP 12-602. *Songs of an Irish Tinker Lady.* Sung by Margaret Barry.

Stinson SLP 72. *Catskill Mountain Folk Songs.* Sung by Bob and Louise DeCormier.

——— SLP 82. *Adirondack Folk Songs and Ballads.* Sung by Milt Okun.

Topic 12T139. *A Wild Bees' Nest: Irish Traditional Ballads.* Sung by Paddy Tunney.

——— 12T140. *A Canadian Garland.* Sung by LaRena Clark. Recorded by Edith Fowke.

——— 12T175. *Willie Clancy, the Minstrel from Clare.* Recorded by Bill Leader.

Index of Song Titles and First Lines

[Song titles are in italics.]